# Contents

# Acknowledgements

This is a book that had to be written and that keeps on having to be read, for the same reason. When my husband died, I searched for someone or something that could assure me I wasn't going insane and that I might survive, a bedside-table book that I could reach for every night (and sometimes during the day) to tell me what I needed to know. This is my bedside-table book. Over the years, it has become the bedside-table book of others who tell me their stories.

This is the twentieth anniversary of the publication of *Beginnings* and this is the fourth update. It's getting to be like a car, needing to be replaced every five years. But not quite. Each time I come back to this book I bring not a new vision but a deeper one, and I pass on a few more insights – mine, and those of the people who share my situation. I'd like to thank all of you who have responded to me and who keep on telling me about your lives and how we have all changed.

Mostly you want to tell me how your husbands died and what your families are doing and how you are coping. One woman, widowed less than a year, told me that her friends kept ordering her to stop dwelling on the past and get on with her life. "Please tell them," she said, "I *am* getting on with it." She was right, of course. Grieving is part of getting on with it.

The Canadian Life and Health Insurance Association originally commissioned a guide for widows that became this book, and I'd like to thank them for their co-operation and interest, specifically Bruce Powe and Isabel Wegg.

*for Bill*

# BEGINNINGS

# 1

## The end and the beginning

*It isn't for the moment you are struck that you need courage, but for the long uphill climb back to sanity and faith and security.*

Anne Morrow Lindbergh

"Every beginning is hard," states a German proverb, and this is no exception. To begin a book with an ending is no way to begin, but this is where you and I come in.

There is no faster way to stop a conversation than to give a straight answer to someone you have just met who asks you, "Where is your husband?" At the moment of truth, the questioner indicates that he wishes the floor would open up and swallow him, and both of you are left at a loss for words. But you might as well get on with it.

Here goes.

My husband was a healthy, vigorous man who took good care of himself. We both worked out three or four times a week at a health club; we watched our weight – he more successfully than I – and we had yearly checkups. At his most recent check-up Bill had been pronounced in excellent condition, cholesterol count low, recovery time good. He was forty-five years old, six foot three, and weighed 175 pounds. On our regular walks we were beginning to look forward to an active old age together. In short, if he were alive today, he'd be a very healthy man.

He burped shortly after Easter Sunday dinner in April, 1973, and died. Death by asphyxiation: the valve in his epiglottis failed to close again after the slight regurgitation, and food got into his windpipe, thence into his lungs and suffocated him within about eight minutes. He didn't know what hit him. Neither did we.

It is not as freaky a death as it might seem; there are statistics on it, and magazine articles are beginning to tell how to prevent such a death. Apparently it is more preventable if food lodges in the windpipe going down than if it sticks there on its way back up. That is merely academic. The fact is that Bill Wylie is dead.

We were having a nice life. We had been married for twenty years, had four children: two girls, Liz and Kate, eighteen and seventeen, and two boys, John and Matthew, fourteen and twelve. Both of us were born in Winnipeg and had moved to Stratford five years earlier when Bill became general manager of the Stratford Festival Theatre. We had a split-level house with a swimming pool in the back yard, a Bassett hound, a cat, a tank full of tropical fish, friends and fun and a future. A nice life.

It changed in a twinkling, as they say, when I turned around and saw his head on the coffee table. He was dead then, though I didn't know it. I gave him mouth-to-mouth resuscitation, but asked my daughter to take over because I thought I must be doing it wrong. There was no response. It was too late. No second chances.

There is a kind of glory in sudden death: to go down at the peak of one's powers with both achievement and potential untarnished, all flags flying. The light is snapped off before it has had a chance to dim or fade. One giant step into the next world. But O pity the survivors! Mid-stride dying is very hard on them. They are left to face the overdue library books, the bouncing cheques (party deceased, funds frozen), the work-in-progress, the plans underway, the gifts on order, all the machinery of daily life that was in full production and that has suddenly stopped. No time to slow down, to re-tool, to lay off. No time to prepare.

There is an Anglican prayer that reads in part, "Preserve us from sudden death." It's a point well taken. Because sudden death does throw a terrible rock into the machinery of normal family living.

No more so, really, than the terrible agony of a terminal illness. That's the way my father went, with cancer, so I've had the dubious privilege of seeing it both ways. It is painful to watch helplessly while someone you love slips away from you. I watched my mother be the eyes and ears and hands of the world her husband was leaving, caring for him with a zeal that almost put her to bed, too. Swift, or agonizingly slow, when death strikes a family, life will never be the same.

Mercifully, one does not immediately realize that fact, however death arrives. First things first. And the first thing on the agenda is a funeral. Funerals are primitive. I always thought so and nothing has changed my mind. And yet, as one friend pointed out, they fulfil the necessary function of convincing everyone that the worst has really happened; he really is dead. And it gives the peripheral friends a chance to do their duty, nevermore to be seen. It's called "paying their respects," and I suppose that fulfils a need as well. Tradition and custom can carry one through an awful lot of swampy territory.

One of the dangers for the widow, though, is that it is done all too swiftly. Speed is not necessarily a good thing. Well-meaning friends are anxious to get every-thing done, arranged, finished, so that you can start getting over it. You don't ever get over it. Loss is perma-nent. Part of you has died, too. So a little wallowing at this time doesn't hurt, if people would only allow it. But our society seems to demand that we behave ourselves at funerals, and after. And we do. Deportment is all. Breakdowns are bad form. But a little howling at the moon might save a lot of tension later on.

One week after my husband's death I was alone with my children. It takes about the same length of time to be left alone with a new baby to bring up. In the latter case, nerves are offset by joy and anticipation. In the silence following the frenzied activity of funeral arrange-ments and people dropping in, the sad fact begins to sink in: life will never be the same again. You are defi-nitely alone. With a lot to learn. As one friend put it: it took me twenty years to learn to live with my husband; I wasn't going to unlearn overnight. Neither will you.

Mourning is a natural and necessary process. It shouldn't be rushed. For in grieving over the loss of another, what we are really doing is grieving over our loss of self, all the self that was invested in that person. We have to get it back somehow.

Freud said that the bereaved has to withdraw her emotional attachment from the deceased. "Withdraw the libido," he said, and, at the same time, begin to "internalize the lost love object." That means letting go, letting go of your husband, without losing your memo-ries of him. You have to build a new relationship with him, and you have to become a new you. It takes time. It can't be hurried.

Grief is an illness with recognizable symptoms. Loss of sleep and loss of appetite contribute effectively to a general exhaustion. There may be headaches, stomach aches, bowel upsets, perhaps even a rash as a result of

14

tension. A dreadful apathy can overtake you, and a withdrawal from reality. Sometimes you can see, more often hear, your husband in another room. For weeks after Bill died I could hear the evening paper rustling as he turned the pages. You lose contact with reality; you lose your trust in life. Death seems much simpler than life and much more welcome. One widow wrote, "I remember I used to think each night as I said my prayers that I was one day nearer the end of my life – and glad of it. That feeling left me."

Note that. The feeling left her. It does, you know. Bereavement is a terrible mental wound, slow to heal, but it does heal. It just takes time. Terrible cliché and not quite true. It also takes hard work. It isn't going to go away all by itself. You have to work at it.

Life, as my oldest daughter said to me, suddenly becomes an uncharted adventure. I found that hard to understand when she said it. I resented it and pushed it away from me. I had been content with my life as it had been, known and charted and secure and happy as it was. Why should I be comforted by the promise of unknown hazards and adventures? And yet, now I see what she meant. How did she know so much?

In his strange and wonderful book *Living Your Dying*, Stanley Keleman hints at the same idea. "Endings," he writes, "bring us face to face with the unknown. Endings force us to make new relationships, or at least offer that opportunity. . . . Many people will say 'that person is irreplaceable to me.' The truth of the matter is that making an ending forces us to start being more self-reliant, or at least offers that opportunity."

No one ever told you it was an opportunity before.

# 2

# From grief to joy

*Joy does not mean riotous glee but it does
mean the purposive employment of energy in a
self-chosen enterprise. It does mean pride and
self-confidence. It does mean communication
and co-operation with others, based on delight
in their company and your own . . . to have
something to desire, to make, to achieve, and
at last something genuine to give.*

*Germaine Greer*

In a death-denying society like ours, the crisis of bereavement is a tough one to face, because no one wants
to let you face it, and no one wants to share it either.

"Cheer up," people say. "You have your children."
Or your memories, or your health, or your money. But
your husband is gone.

"Pull yourself together," they say. "There are worse
things than death." They're right, of course, but name
one.

"Stiff upper lip," they say. "He wouldn't want to see

you like this." What's so bad about a quivering lower one? I'd like there to be a little breast-beating when I go, just to let me know I was missed.

"Carry on," they say. "You have to get up and keep going." Why?

In all other cases of shock, we are told the recommended treatment is rest and warmth. Pile on the blankets and the comfort. Why should it be any different for the shock of death? An electric blanket may be a poor substitute for a husband, but at a time like this it's the closest thing to the womb there is – a place to retreat to and lick one's wounds.

Psychologists have only recently recognized the deep needs of the survivor, and the patterns that grief must take if one is to recover and go on living a meaningful life. The whole process is described as "grief work," and it is very hard work. No part of it can be shirked. If it is, it will have to be faced and gone through at a later date, often with severe complications. After the initial, blessed numbness has worn off, there are hostility and guilt and depression to be worked through before any acceptance can be achieved.

Roughly classified, the stages of grief may be described as shock, denial, and acceptance, but a more detailed analysis may prove to be of some value. You'll find a number of variations depending on whose book you read, but here is a fairly comprehensive list:

I    Shock
      1. Initial shock
      2. Emotional release
      3. Loneliness

II   Denial
      1. Depression
      2. Panic
      3. Hostility

4. Guilt
5. Inability to return to normal activity

III    Acceptance
1. Gradual hope
2. Struggle to affirm reality

The whole process can take well over a year, and there is always the chance after that of an unpredictable relapse when some unexpected, heartbreakingly simple commonplace suddenly reduces you to helpless tears. Bear with it. These symptoms do not necessarily follow the order of my neat column, nor does everyone suffer all of them. But they may serve as a guide to the kinds of emotions a widow must work through to earn her wings (not angel wings – wings of hope). The comfort in confronting such a list is the realization that you are not alone. Others have gone this path before you as there will be others after you. I know. I've been that way myself.

The psychiatrist Dr. Thomas Holmes has listed those life events that cause stress in human beings, with a stress-rating for each event. The event with the highest number of stress points is the death of a spouse with a box score of 100; next on the list is divorce with a score of 75. Holmes's idea is that no one should accumulate a life stress score of more than 200 in any given twelve-month period. A higher score can lead to serious illness, injury, or accidents. This is why one of the best pieces of advice a recent widow can listen to is: "Don't do anything rash."

Even if she doesn't do anything, there are changes that accompany the loss of her husband which automatically add to her stress. A change in financial status carries a score of 38; her finances have automatically undergone a change, and she won't be certain how she's fixed for a few months. Change to a different line of work is worth 36 points, or a business readjustment is 39. Within the year, if she wasn't working before, it's likely she will start now. If she was working, there are still subtle differences: she is the sole breadwinner now and it changes the job as well as the person doing it. A change in work responsibility is worth 29. Changes in eating (15) and sleeping habits (16) also account for stress points, and these changes are impossible to avoid.

One widow assured me it would be six months before I would be able to taste food or sleep through the night. Another one, older, said it would be a year. I wouldn't say my sleeping habits have ever recovered.

I was always the last one to bed. Bill was the one who locked the doors, put the milk order out and the cat in the basement, and turned out the lights around me until I said, "Hey, wait for me!" Now I try, I do try, to get to bed at a reasonable hour – and then I write in bed. But if something happens to hook me, like a book, or a list, or a new idea, it's game over. I'm up till 3 or 4 A.M. and sleep seems a waste of time.

A change in social life also causes stress (18 points), and it's more than that. As you get cut out of the social stream, resentment increases, and that brings a stress of its own. Special events, even happy ones, bring stress to everyone. Christmas carries a score of 12, and the first one A.D. must carry a little more than that. In these stressful times, it's not hard to pile up a sizable score even without a Super Event to send it soaring. Each family has its own events which will add to the strain. My first child left home to go off to university within that first year – that's 29 points. One divorcée asked me what was the score if your oldest unmarried daughter had an abortion. Holmes didn't cover that one. You can see that even if you don't do anything, you have enough stress to work through without going out of your way to find some more.

That's why I say for at least a year, sit tight. Work through your grief. Don't add moving or other major changes to the already drastic change in your life, if you can possibly help it.

You have a lot of emotions, reflexes, and habits tied up in one person, and they have to be released before you go on. Mary Vachon, who used to be a mental health consultant with the Clarke Institute in Toronto, describes your task this way: "You have to get back a lot of the emotion you invested in the dead person." She also says that the 37 per cent widowed under the age of sixty-five are the worst problem area; that is, they represent a high-risk group. Some of the facts the Clarke Institute discovered during its research illustrate the high-risk factor of widows in specific age brackets. For instance, in the year following the death of their husbands, the young widows studied experienced three times as many hospital admissions as other women of similar age. The widows studied experienced a 12 per cent increase in mortality during the first year of bereavement. And 32 per cent of widows suffer "marked deterioration in health" within thirteen months after their husbands' deaths compared to 2 per cent for the control group.

Mary Vachon listed the types of cases with the greatest risk factor:

1. those with poor social support;
2. those under forty-five whose husbands died suddenly; or, conversely, those over sixty-five, whose husbands suffered a lingering death;
3. those with an ambivalent relationship to the deceased (those who have the most difficulty recovering are those who had the worst marriages);
4. those who were denied the grief experience because of minimal funeral ceremonies;

5. those with previous psychiatric difficulties. (If they were suicidal before, their chances of death by suicide are greatly increased; suicide is a high risk for the first five years following a spouse's death.)

Like most widows I know, I behaved myself during the initial impact. I had an ulcer that did tend to stand at attention under stress, though, so my doctor deemed it advisable to give me a relaxant to keep my gut from taking me on an acid trip. It was mild, however, and used sparingly. I was fully aware of what I was doing and why. I have since heard of widows whose doctors thought they were doing them a favour by tranquillizing them out of their skulls during the first after-days of shock. I do not believe in such a practice, trying to turn a pill into a twentieth-century balm of Gilead. Nor do I believe in the indiscriminate use of sleeping pills. If you are fortunate enough to have a religious faith, you will find that prayer does much more than Nembutal.

One widow told me, "My electric blanket saved me." Me too. I used to turn it and the bedside lamp on long before bedtime, so that when I was finally ready to try to sleep, the light and warmth would welcome me. Sleep does return in time, though perhaps your sleep patterns will have changed. All your other patterns will have changed; why should sleep be different?

Use the time. Other widows besides me – and not necessarily writers – have used paper in the wee small hours of the night to keep them company and sane. With me it began with my sympathy letters – some 700 of them. I wrote long into the night, every night, for weeks and weeks, replying at length to each letter I had received. This, of course, kept me from facing that empty (but warm) bed.

I began to keep a diary every night. It was a substitute for my bedtime conversation with Bill. It also proved to be a wonderful release (note stage 2 in the list of recovery symptoms above). Emotional release comes in many different forms. Welcome them all, because you need them. Paper helps dry the tears. Tears will come, of course, and must not be denied. But sometimes, when the pain is too overwhelming, it helps to distance it a little, or at least set it slightly aside, by writing down what you feel.

I didn't always wait till bedtime. If something really got to me, I'd rush to my diary and write it all down. A lot of the early pages are tear-splattered, but ballpoint pens don't run. I think it's better to run to paper than to a tranquillizer. In my case it's almost as addictive, but there are fewer side effects.

I have since recommended a journal to a number of people, not necessarily widows, who were depressed. "Write it down," I say. "Get it on paper, and take a look at it." All who have tried it report that it helps.

Since then I realized I was not alone in my tendency to turn to paper. When I began to explore other women's (published) diaries, I learned that others like myself have considered a private journal the safest and most salutary method of giving way to their emotions. For some reason, you'll find that other people's expressions of grief can be very comforting. I'll include a few such books in the bibliography. I'm still addicted to the habit myself; it's one of my ways of surviving solitude. My diary is my comfortable companion. Try it and see.

It's not only grief you may want to express. If you do get angry or resentful at people's treatment of you, at real or fancied slights, you can write it all down, let off all your steam, without saying anything you might be sorry for later. If, like me, you are a this-time-last-year kind of person, you can indulge in that to your heart's content, without boring anyone. Go ahead and dwell on your milestones. Recall – and write down – the happy times as well as the bad ones. Set yourself assignments. Thanksgiving is a good place to start. Each Thanksgiving I make a point of thinking of and writing down all the things I have to be thankful for. Work at it. Don't take anything for granted. Realize how blessed you are, and count your blessings by writing them down. Then, later, on a day when you've hit a low ebb, go back and read what you've written. That will help. You have just become your own therapist. Never underestimate the power of paper! Consider your diary your Withdrawal Book. And don't worry if you can't spell; no one's going to see it but you.

It's hard sometimes to distinguish between genuine grief and self-pity. "Our tears are selfish," wrote Peter Marshall in his book of sermons, *Mr. Jones, Meet the Master*, "for we are self-centred – self-absorbed. We keep thinking of what it means to us. We reflect how much we miss the departed, and we weep because we begrudge their going. We wish they had stayed on with us awhile. . . . We wish things had gone on as they were. We resent the change, somehow, never thinking what it must mean to them that are gone."

Self-pity is a kind of permissive self-dramatization. And grief is very like fear. "Perhaps," says C.S. Lewis, "more strictly, like suspense. Or like waiting; just hanging about waiting for something to happen. It gives life a permanently provisional feeling." Grief is an agonized apprehension of something that has already happened. It's standing at the edge of a void, a very recently carved hole that has forced a change in your direction. It is knowing, with a sinking feeling in your gut, that you have to go on, alone, and that's painful.

Pain takes many different forms. If you can let self-pity give way to irony, there's hope for you yet. One of my children gave me the best example to follow. John, at fourteen, went off to his beloved summer camp as planned. One night at camp a group of boys was sitting around a campfire talking, John told me later, and they began to compare notes on their fathers' occupations. "What does your dad do?" John had no intention of telling them his father had died two months before; that would involve a singling-out he didn't want. When it came his turn to say what his father did, he said casually, "Well, he lies around a lot."

I remember my refusal of a gift of lilacs the first spring A.D. because my husband was allergic to them. It took me weeks to stop heading for the passenger side of the car, and over two years before I ever spread out in the double bed – there was a small neat dent where I carefully slept on my side, though I always turned on the blanket on his side, in case a stray leg got chilled in the night. The first roast I attempted to carve caused a few tears and some messy chunks of meat. Fortunately, roast beef is so expensive now we don't have the problem very often. It is not, in fact, for the predictably difficult situations that you must brace yourself, but for the simple events that can undo you. I was visiting friends and saw the wife slip a lipstick in her husband's pocket – all the preparation she needed to go out, since he had the money, identification, car and house keys. I used to do that too, and I can't any more. That hurt. But these are examples of self-pity – easy traps – and not to be tolerated.

The panic associated with the depression of loneliness (see list again) seems to come when you are expected to do something you have always let your husband do because he did it so much better. We women have all been pampered and protected into a state of near-incompetence. If feminism gives women a stronger

24

sense of self, a larger competence in financial and mechanical matters, a greater confidence in their own ability to cope with life's practical problems, then it will ease the role of widows everywhere. The first time I had to back into a parking place in a car park I realized anew that I was alone. There was no one to do it for me; I had to do it myself. I did, of course. Out of that initial panic rose determination and, eventually, skill. Now I can squeeze back into spaces that you wouldn't believe.

And then you hit another aspect of the loneliness. When you do achieve something, you have no one to share it with. Your loving reflector is gone. As one widower put it to me, "I know well the temptations of self-pity and the danger of enjoying sympathy. These come, I think, because that special understanding, so generously given and so esteeming, has abruptly gone, and there remains a struggle not to shrink and become less of a person. Widow and widower are so terribly vulnerable."

Depression is a form of anger. The loss of a loved one generates a lot of hostility which must be worked through. Often the hostility is directed at the person who died. The widow feels she has been unfairly abandoned, and it's all his fault. All the if-onlies are his fault. I know one widow who told me that every time she hit a crisis during the first year following her husband's death she'd address him aloud: "John Smith," she'd shout, "why did you leave me to face this alone?"

If the marriage was less than ideal, a terrible guilt accompanies the anger. The survivor feels guilty that she wasn't nicer, more patient, more forgiving, more loving. Whatever faults her spouse threw at her in their bad scenes, she hurls at herself with a cruel ferocity. Fine. Let it all happen. All those emotions have to be recovered and worked out.

Psychiatrist Karen Horney treated anger: she pointed out that we cannot deal with our anger unless we allow it to enter our consciousness. You have to recognize it and you mustn't be afraid of it. Maturity isn't denying anger, it's facing it. Repressing anger is dangerous, as is repressing grief. You have been deeply wounded, and you must act before gangrene sets in.

Anger is caused by some frustration – in this case, your husband's death – which has thwarted your hopes and plans for a future that included him in it. If you're not angry at him, then you turn your anger on others for frustrating you; for ignoring you, you think; for forgetting you; for not making a fuss over you; for excluding you; in short, for going on living their own lives.

To rid yourself of anger you must either remove the obstacles in the path of your frustration or recognize what these obstacles are and change your expectations. Well, you can't remove the death. But you can recognize the gap between your expectations and people's performance, and do one or several things about that.

1. Close the gap. Be more realistic in your expectations. Realistic, not cynical.
2. In the case of genuine slights, rebuffs, or disappointments, shrug your shoulders and give up. Write them off. It happens. "I've lost the Soanso's," I moaned to a friend. "No," my friend said, "they've lost you."
3. Concentrate on the goodies. Play the Glad Game. Marvel at the unlooked-for, unexpected kindnesses people have done you. Say it out loud. Write it down. Count your blessings. Keep counting.
4. When you cannot remove the cause of your anger, when it's permanent, as in this case, then find extra energy in yourself to cope with it.

Direct that energy into a creative, satisfying outlet: a sport, a hobby, a volunteer job, a new project at work. Make your anger-energy work for you!

Some people get angry at God. But as one widow told me, "I think He's big enough to handle it."

In my case, I felt neither hostility nor guilt. My husband died such a sudden, freakish death that I could hardly blame him for leaving. He must have been as astonished as I was. And our marriage was so satisfying that it left nothing unsaid or undone. I'd have liked years more of it, mind you, but it was complete. Sometimes I now think, maybe we had it all, and that's why it ended. Who knows? But my depression did turn into anger. I was angry at most of my friends. I demanded more of them than anyone could possibly deliver, and since people don't deliver much to widows, there was quite a gap between their delivery and my expectations. If only we could tell people the kind of help we need and expect.

At first we need someone to talk to, to pour it all out at, to go over the details of our life and his death until we have it all together and begin to accept it as reality and not some nightmare we may eventually waken from.

Next, we need someone to count on, some semblance of routine. Activity really does help, and widows left with children at home are fortunate in the sense that they have people they must do something for. A friend can, however, offer a regular visit or a planned activity to look forward to and count on for a few weeks or months.

A friend can also help with that next phase in our little list: inability to return to normal activity. It was a good friend who made me return to our weekly swimming class at the Y, and who made me have our annual swimming party at the end of the season. It was my own common sense that made me return to the church choir sooner than anyone else recommended.

When death has reduced "normal" to a meaningless word, any semblance of normal routine is a great help. Anything that gives you some kind of focus can help to keep you sane in those first terrible months of re-adjustment. That's why work can be a blessing. Gradually, unbidden, stray streamers of hope lighten the darkness. You know now it's not a case of getting over, it's getting through it.

Happiness is not a pursuit in itself and does not come on command. Happiness is a by-product which sneaks up on you, unsought, when you're busy at something else. Joy, on the other hand, is a positive activity, one that is every person's duty to cultivate. I believe you must work at joy. Demand it as your right; pursue it as your goal; give it to others as your obligation to them.

One of the first things you can do, as you look around in your increasing light, is find someone else who needs help. One widow wrote me: "A source of strength is either to phone or go to see someone who is in far worse straits – and one does not have to look far." There are self-help programs operating here and there across the country, widows helping widows, and that's not a bad place to begin.

Only widows, or, if one is lucky, one's closest friends, can know what another widow is going through. It's a sisterhood with terrible dues, a membership you would avoid if you could. Once arrived, however, your capacity for compassion and sympathy and practical help expands enormously. Heart and hands reach out to help others in pain and need. And this, perhaps, is the greatest affirmation of reality a person can achieve.

# 3

# Changing your lifestyle

*The most difficult adjustment a woman
is called on to make is learning to live alone
after being married.*

Isabella Taves

A widow is not immediately aware of how different her life is. At first the changes seem minute. You go on in the house. You stick to the routine, especially if you have children. You do what must be done each day – cleaning, cooking, shopping. Familiar tasks are a blessing and a comfort. It's almost as if your husband were away on an extended business trip. Almost. There is less laundry, of course. The pressure of producing a great dinner every night, if you ever felt such a pressure, eases. Your social life drops like a stone.

The first thing you notice is that you have a lot more time on your hands. There is no one to coax you to have another cup of coffee, a drink, a chat, a walk. You seem to have become more efficient, but time hangs heavy. What do you want to save it for?

Little by little, though, the changes become more

apparent and more drastic. It's as if the two of you had been arrows shot from two bows, your paths parallel. The event that stopped the flight of one arrow has deflected the path of yours. Little by little, the trajectory will be greatly changed. You're flying on alone. What happens, ultimately, is that your whole lifestyle changes.

This is a secret that your friends and acquaintances know before you do: you are a different person. External circumstances are going to force changes in you that you never expected. It's irrelevant whether or not you wanted them; they're going to happen. Life has written you a new script.

Since your future has changed so much, you might as well get ready for it by taking a long hard look at your life right now. Everything you have been accustomed to doing bears scrutiny and re-evaluation. Start by questioning your daily routine. Why are you doing what you do in the way that you do it? Habit? Or necessity? For whom are you running your household now? What are your priorities?

You were probably running the house for your husband before. Dinner was set in accordance with the time he came home. Your shopping and free time were arranged to accommodate your social life together. If you worked as well, then you had, no doubt, reciprocal arrangements and divisions of labour, but it was team work. Everything you did was done with someone else's needs in mind. Marriage, we are told, is supposed to be an equal partnership, but some partnerships are more equal than others. And in most cases the older the widow, the more male-dominated the household was. Most marriages in this century and on this continent have acknowledged the male as the head of the household. Life With Father is a twentieth-century truism.

Now that Father isn't there, it's time you took a good

look at yourself. Otherwise you're going to atrophy like Queen Victoria. Everyone knows the story of her devoted grief, how the room was kept as it always was, and Albert's clothes laid out every day. No one expects or admires that kind of paralysis on the part of a widow today.

Speaking of clothes, you should remove your husband's clothes from your house as soon as possible. It is more important that he take a permanent place in your heart and memory than be revered in a moth-eaten sweater. I gave shirts to nephews, underwear and socks and pyjamas to the Salvation Army, and sold the good suits to a second-hand clothing store. The beautiful ties, which my husband collected and prized, I gave away to his closest men friends, to remember him by, at least as long as they were in style. Empty the closet and open your heart.

And stay open. You're going to have to keep an open mind if you're going to change, and you have to change, though slowly at first. Little by little you realize you don't have to cater to other people's needs all the time; in fact, it's time you started paying some attention to your own. You're the only one who's going to.

And that's the next step to total assessment. You begin to take a look at all your habits, and you start to analyze how you got that way, why you do this or that, and you begin to question the necessity of continuing in the same – not pattern – rut.

The first changes are the hardest and the most exciting – even simple ones like shifting shopping times or your laundry habits. Your cooking habits change, too, and not always for the better. The widow living alone has the biggest problem in the kitchen. I read recently that a single person pays at least 20 per cent more for food because of the inability to buy in quantity at lower prices. Even one tin of something lasts two or three meals, and boredom sets in, accompanied by a lack of appetite. My father, a doctor, used to say that women living alone subsisted on a diet of tea and toast and corn flakes – "No fit food," he used to say, "for growing females." The widow living alone should try to maintain good eating habits to ensure her health. If that sounds too preachy, I'm sorry. But you have a long time to go on alone; you might as well do it in good health.

One of the hidden bonuses of being single is that you are in control. You make the decisions now, so don't be afraid to experiment. Why not have soup for breakfast (or good old-fashioned porridge), or a gigantic baked potato loaded with salsa or cottage cheese and chopped green onions, and maybe a salad for dinner? Make a point, if you can afford it, of having a guest at least once a week, for lunch or dinner, or for coffee and dessert. It's not only good for your morale and your appetite, but if you choose your guest wisely, it will also result in a return invitation, which is even better for the morale and the appetite.

Cooking presents different problems to the working mother, to the scrimping housewidow, and to the lonely, older widow. Each situation, however, is sure to be different from what it was before. As a working mother you have to be sure your children are getting the best nutrition possible with the least amount of effort and maximum efficiency on your part. Obviously, you can't spend hours in the kitchen fussing about food. At the same time, you can't simply broil a fast chop every night. That's too expensive, and dull. There never has been a time when more information was available for whatever problem has to be handled. The libraries and bookstores are crammed with cookbooks, and there are a lot of them dedicated to casseroles, do-ahead foods, the specific problems of a working cook, or cooking for one or two. Similarly, if money is a problem – and when isn't it? – there are cookbooks that tell you how to get the most nutrition, fun, and good taste for your food dollars.

Surveys have indicated that women without men do not set as good a table as they did. The image you had of yourself as Earth Mother, Hostess Bountiful, Giver of All Good Things to Eat, seems to have disappeared. The reasons are understandable enough. You don't have the same incentive that you did. You've lost your most appreciative audience. You don't have as much money. Lots of reasons. Old Mother Hubbard's cupboard was bare – it's obvious she was a widow.

This change is almost imperceptible as it happens; it creeps up on you by degrees. As a matter of fact, until I moved, I kept on running a household for six, even though two and then three of the occupants were no longer with us. My oldest daughter went off to university the fall after my husband died, followed by my second daughter the year after. I had three fridges and a freezer, and I seemed to keep on filling them, though I must admit I had more trouble emptying them than before. It wasn't until I was in a three-bedroom apartment with one refrigerator that I began buying and cooking for three instead of six, and that's when I found I couldn't always have an extra one or two for dinner on short notice. Of course, that wasn't the only reason. My typewriter, by that time, was far more important to me than my food processor, and now my word processor has progressed to a state-of-the-art computer that occupies my waking thoughts. You see, changes sneak up on you, whether you are aware of them or not.

The way you spend your time changes more than the way you set your table. The absence of your husband changes the way you spend almost every moment of your life, especially the moments you used to spend together. Times when you are most empty and unoccupied, like the

33

hour before dinner when he used to come home and talk over the day, or Saturday night which you used to spend together – these are the very times when your married friends are busiest with their husbands. You must fill that time for yourself.

The dinner hour is the easiest to fill. You simply move it forward; you don't have to wait for anyone to come home, and kids are always happy to eat early. It gives you a longer evening, but you'll learn to fill that productively, and even be grateful for the time. If you're working, there's less problem with empty times on weekdays. You'll be too busy to notice when you have to do everything yourself.

I know a lot of widows who write letters, pay their bills, and balance their budgets on Saturday nights. Other nights it is possible to find single things to do – meetings to go to, activities to occupy yourself – but Saturday seems to be couple-oriented, like the society we live in. If you want to be occupied on Saturday night, you're going to have to plan ahead. As a matter of fact, all singles have to do a great deal of planning ahead. You don't have a built-in companion for whatever spontaneous activity comes to mind.

I have on occasion gone out to dinner on a Saturday night with a wrench of widows, but I don't recommend this as common practice. Tickets for many events are more expensive on Saturdays, and restaurants are usually more crowded. It doesn't matter that there are five or six of you, if you're all female, the waiter says, "Oh, you're alone," and puts you near the kitchen door. Buy a VCR if you don't already have one and rent a couple of movies. If you make enough noise with your popcorn, you might not notice you're alone.

Sunday is white-knuckle day. It helps to go to church, if you are that way inclined (I was). Some working mothers find it helps to sleep in. If you're a working

34

mother you may be doing the laundry and other house-hold chores on Sunday afternoon. This is often more productive and less depressing than a walk. Walking is best with two. But keep exercising.

For a while I tried to fill Sundays by having guests for dinner, either whole families that my children would enjoy, or singles that they could help to entertain. It gave us all a focus, I thought, to concentrate on some-one outside ourselves on Sunday afternoon. It helps – for a while. If you have been accustomed to cooking a good Sunday dinner, you won't feel the pressure of having "company" as much. If you look around, you can find any number of waifs and strays who would enjoy a Sunday dinner. There are lots of singles around who are as lonely as you are. In fact, singles are better than families. You don't expect them to reciprocate.

After one season I quit having people for Sunday dinner. No one ever asked us back – that's how it grad-ually dawned on me that my friends had changed. Don't dwell on it when it happens to you. Accept what has happened and move on. Anyway, company for Sunday dinner became less and less attractive because (a) it's expensive, and (b) it's tiring. There are some weeks you just don't have the time or energy to make a special dessert.

You will find, as time goes by, that the people you have over and the people who invite you to their homes differ from the people you used to see when you were part of a couple. That's the way it goes. You are a dif-ferent person now, and you're not the only one who has learned how different you are. One plus one equalled a couple before, and you and your husband moved easily among a group of friends who considered you a unit. Like Mutt and Jeff. Ham and eggs. But in the eyes of the world, or at least of the society you live in, two take away one doesn't equal one. Most of the time it equals nothing. Face it: you are odd woman out. Very few people want seven or nine or eleven, let alone thirteen, at their dinner tables. Most people think you'd rather not come alone to their parties. They think tickets come in even numbers.

The remarkable thing is that other people change faster than you do. You still cling to the idea that you are a person, a human being in your own right. No one else does. You are going to have to change their minds for them, and in the process you will undergo a few changes yourself.

Never mind. If you're forgotten when it comes to playtime, you're Number One on the list when it comes to work – unpaid, of course. I mean, you have all that time on your hands. The first fall after my husband's death I was not invited out to dinner but I was asked to run a publicity campaign for the local Y, bake pies for the church bake sale, sell books for the Y book sale, canvass for the United Appeal, be an area manager for a fund-raising drive, and fill in on short notice as a fourth at bridge. I hate bridge.

Maybe what people do to you actually helps while it hurts. It hurts at the time but you begin to learn the hard way that you really are alone. As my first Christmas A.D. approached, one of my closest friends said to me, "I'd invite you all for dinner on Christmas but you have to face reality sooner or later." I thought I had been facing reality for six months, daily. Suttee, the practice whereby the widow throws herself on her husband's funeral pyre, has been outlawed in India. They still practise a subtle form of it in Canada. You die by inches, of loneliness.

If you think I'm being too bitter or grim or harsh, bear with me. I'm stating the facts first, in their plainest terms. There are, of course, wonderful exceptions, sources of help and comfort you never expected – and often not from the friends you have relied on over the years. A drastic change has occurred in your life, and it sets off a chain reaction of changes all the way down the line, in friends and family and society, as well as in your whole lifestyle.

Well, that's as bad as it gets. From here on in, you have nowhere to go but up. It's a long climb but you have lots of time, and you have an asset no one, maybe even you, realizes. Yourself. If you weren't before, you are about to become your own best friend.

Having told you the worst, let me now reassure you. There never has been a time in history when it has been more exciting to be a single woman. One of the better long-term effects of the feminist movement is the opportunity it has given a single woman to make a new life for herself as a vital, functioning, contributing person. It is still up to you, of course, but others have stuck their feet in doors for you. The future is yours in a way that it never has been before. Whether you find that challenging or frightening depends on you.

If friends invite you somewhere – anywhere! – say yes. Don't give them the excuse not to ask you next time because "you'd only say no anyway." They find their own reasons quickly enough. If you're working and there's an office party, go to it. You may end up on sandwich detail or the punch bowl, but go. If you're invited to a wedding and you have no one to go with, go anyway – and that goes for cocktail and any other kinds of parties, dinners, theatre performances, home-and-school or annual meetings, political rallies, anything. Go! You will find you have to draw some lines at volunteer work because the invitations in this area are endless. You need to decide where you will devote your energy and time and where your saturation point is, because it's in you, not in the work to be done.

One of the things I didn't know I knew, I learned from my widowed mother and aunts whom I had unconsciously observed before I became a widow myself. I watched these widows say no and dwindle. Mind you, they were a lot older than I was, and it was harder for them to say yes. Saying yes means making an effort, spending some energy, and maybe even some money, and taking risks. So my motto as a widow is: "Never say no to anything – within reason!" I have ended up in some peculiar situations because of this, and I have had some rotten times. But I have also had some unexpectedly good times and met a few really enjoyable people I might not otherwise have met. As a newly single person, you have to keep meeting new people, you see, because a lot of your old relationships are no longer valid. You are the one who's changing, though it seems at first that other people have.

Some friends may forget you at the dinner table, but I have found that a single woman is far more welcome as a house guest than a couple. A single woman can fit in the spare room, help with the kids, pitch in with the cooking, and adapt to any plans going on in a busy, active household far more readily than a couple.

Travel is a wonderful form of escape. Every widow I know will go anywhere at the drop of a hat or a ticket. I have never refused any trip or visit that is offered me and I have been the grateful recipient of food, drink, hospitality, and even airline tickets from dear, kind, generous friends.

I still feel alien on this planet without my husband. Somehow, when I am away from home, I feel less strange, in a perverse sort of way. I mean, I'd be foreign anyway. And I like the feeling of being suspended in space and time, of having, for the time being, no real responsibilities, no commitments, no pressures. So often, since Bill died, I have asked myself in wonder, "What am I doing here?" When I'm on a trip I know the answer. I'm visiting.

So I have travelled a lot since his death and rarely stay in hotel rooms. I have learned how to be a guest, and I have become closer friends with my long-distance friends and their children than I might ever have had the opportunity to be otherwise.

I like flying alone. I like driving alone. It took me longer to get used to going to movies or the theatre alone. Everyone has a threshold of intolerance she must surmount and that was mine. For a long time I sought a few friends, those with busy husbands or none at all who liked movies as much as I do, and I went with them. Now I have learned to slip gracefully into a supper show alone (preferably on the reduced-price day). I guess the first time I managed to get a single orchestra seat for a Broadway hit changed my attitude to attending the theatre alone. In any case, I am more aggressive about theatre. I get myself a single ticket and offer dinner before or drinks and supper after to a couple I know is also going. Or I get two or three tickets and offer myself as a package deal. This usually results in dinner on the man or the couple – but rarely on another woman. Women go Dutch, no matter who bought the tickets. (Don't you be like that.)

The point is that anything is possible; you just have to plan a little more. One single complained to me that life had become once again one long series of dates.

It's true. You have to plan ahead. It takes money and time and energy to maintain a social life, and all three have decreased for the widow. It's a whole new ball-game, and it requires a whole new set of ground rules. You start by trying to fill in lonely gaps – the dinner hour, Saturday nights, Sundays. You progress to theatre-going, travel, new interests, maybe even, in time, new men. But we'll get to that later.

Brace yourself. You have to develop a single psyche again. As one friend said to me, "Just remember you're

39

not married any more." It's painful, but it bears repeating, because after all these years of marriage, it's hard to remember.

As you go on, you see, the changes get both easier and more drastic. You change your emphasis. You realize that people are more important than things, that your children are more important than your routine, that you are more important than conventional habits.

Habit is a comfortable skin that cushions a lot of shocks. Shedding the skin can be painful. Change is always painful. But you have had the biggest change of your life thrust upon you. No choice. If you don't change to meet it, you won't survive.

# 4

# Coping with money

*Money may not be important but it
quiets the nerves.*

*Joe E. Lewis*

Wherever I go to speak or to read from my work, no
matter the subject, women come up to me to talk about
*Beginnings*. They carry a fresh, crisp copy sent to them
by their husband's insurance company or a tattered,
dog-eared book lent to them by a widowed friend. (I
wish I had a nickel for every time the book has been
loaned and returned and loaned again!) First editions
are treasured not because they are collectors' items but
because they are still in use. As I sign their book, women
ask me questions:

- Is it still possible to roll the Widow's Allowance
  into an RRSP? (No)
- Can you still get the mortgage holder to waive the
  penalty if you pay off the house with insurance
  money? (Many women make a point of telling me

41

they have done this, following my advice. The answer is: It doesn't hurt to ask.)

- Should you move? (Not in the first year, if you can avoid it.)
- What should I do about those RSVPs? (I can't answer that in a single sentence.)
- How do you make ends meet when the ends are growing farther apart? (This question is the reason Lynne MacFarlane and I wrote *Everywoman's Money Book*.)

The questions always have to do with practical difficulties. My emotional facts are timeless. But the day-to-day business of life changes, and that's why you are now reading a new chapter on coping with money. Tax laws, insurance products, investment strategies, real estate values, interest rates, and the cost of living all shift and vary and fluctuate over the years. Your need for a practical game plan does not. What you have to develop is a functional, generic, non-obsolescent approach.

In other updates I have inserted addenda: relevant tax, insurance, and financial tips as times and governments change over the years and our leaders' not-so-wise and often ill-considered arrangements affect our lives; emotional facts of life picked up as I grew older and experienced first-hand the joy and pain of single sex, the rueful sweetness of single grandparenthood, the wistful observation of other women's husbands in retirement – my most recent discovery. Of course, I have incised and inserted new insights and updates elsewhere in this book as well, but I have written this chapter in the hope that you will develop your own pragmatic survival skills, good for the rest of your life.

Let's deal with income first. Women's economic circumstances have improved slightly in the past twenty years. Although well over half of all adult Canadian women – married or not, childless or not – are working, they are still not paid as well as men. At the rate the gap is closing, I figure we'll reach pay equity by the year 2030, too late to do most of us any good. At least those of you who have been working outside the home will have earned some Canada Pension money by the time you reach retirement age. Women in the work force have been able to contribute a percentage of their earned income to their own Registered Retirement Savings Plans (RRSPs), which will give them a little nest egg to hatch in their twilight years. Spousal Plans, for wives without earned money, are less popular because they must be funded by husbands (statistics indicate that often the money for spousal RRSPs comes from the woman's purse: saved or inherited money). Some women have learned/are learning about investments; the relative safety and ease of mutual funds have given them a taste for dividends. A widow can inherit her husband's Canada Pension, though halved (divorcées, too, are entitled to a share of their ex's CPP).

The Widow's and Orphan's Allowance, part of CPP (and QPP in Quebec, with slightly different rules), is still available for widows thirty-five and older whose husbands contributed to CPP. It pays a taxable death benefit as well as a monthly allowance to the widow and to each minor dependant, and to unmarried children between eighteen and twenty-five years of age, paid directly to them on proof of their attendance at a recognized institution of learning. CPP also has a disability benefit. If the deceased qualified for a disability payment, the children are entitled to receive a survivor's benefit, with the same qualifications applying if they are over eighteen and under twenty-five.

The Widow's Allowance must be applied for, accompanied by documents necessary to establish the applicant's claim. These include the following:

1. The death certificate. Apply for copies (at least ten, as you'll find you need them) to the Registrar of your province. The funeral director will supply you with an application form. The coroner's report goes automatically to the Registrar's office, so all you need is money. The amount, of course, goes up over the years. Send a money order; I don't trust certified cheques in the mail.
2. your husband's birth certificate,
3. his social insurance card,
4. your marriage certificate (and your divorce papers, if any),
5. your birth certificate,
6. your children's birth certificates,
7. your social insurance card,
8. your children's social insurance cards, if any,
9. your husbands' last income tax return, with its statement of contributory salary and wages (don't throw away his tax returns for five years!).

Once you have all these papers together, it's a good idea to keep them in a safe place, because you'd be amazed at how often you have to refer to them. (I carry my birth certificate in my wallet, as I'm sure you do.) One married friend told me that when she read this list she collected everything and put it in a small safe that she keeps under her bed. She told me her husband was a bit worried when she explained to him what it was for, but it gave her peace of mind!

Paperwork is not difficult, but it's fiddly. An enormous amount of it can be done by phone, finding out what you need to know and gather and what you can submit by mail. Look up the Blue Pages in your phone book and consult the relevant government department. (Income Security is probably the one you'll refer to most often.) Have pencil and paper handy to make a list. You can have application forms sent to you, then fill them out and send them back. Your local post office has some forms (for example, passport renewal) and your local postmaster is legally qualified to notarize or witness anything you need to have signed. You might find it convenient, as I have, to arrange – on yet another form – for any government cheques (CPP, OAS, etc.) to be deposited directly into your bank account instead of being mailed to you. It's a comforting feeling to know that on a certain day each month your account will burgeon, and it saves you a trip to the bank or the danger of losing a cheque (it happens).

While we're mentioning banks, I do hope you had your own personal account as well as a joint account. Most joint accounts have a right of survivorship, giving the surviving half of a joint couple free access to what's in there, but it's a good idea for each half of any pair to have an individual account as well. Tell your friends.

At the time of writing, the Old Age Security payment still functions without a means test and almost automatically. You have to write a reminder to the government four or five months before you turn sixty-five to receive a birthday present when you reach your seniority, proving your claim with your birth certificate. As with passports, always send this document by registered mail. In addition, there is still a Guaranteed Income Supplement for those seniors whose income falls below what Stats Canada euphemistically calls the LICO, that is, Low Income Cut-Off (read: poverty line). I say *still* in all these instances because government cushions are wearing thin sooner than we'd like, making life a little tougher for Canadians as they grow older, especially single ones.

Early retirement (a euphemism for unemployment) on the one hand and a raised retirement age on the other – for receipt of CPP or Old Age disbursements; means tests; fixed payments no longer pegged to inflation rates and rising costs; all these threats of attrition accompany the already-realized perils of the Senior Benefits Program. The eligible age for contributions to an RRSP has been cut from seventy-one to sixty-nine, the time when all moneys accrued must be rolled over into some appropriate income vehicle. Those three years (cut-off is effective at the end of the year in which you reach the magic number) of further investment and compound interest all without tax would have made a serious difference in your ultimate income.

Of course, there are private sources of income. Private pension plans are decreasing in number, but those in effect are still heavily weighted in favour of men: women are cut in later, leave sooner, lose valuable years of accrual if they take time off for children, and at pay-out time are penalized with smaller payments because they tend to live longer. The law now requires that retiring husbands have their wives' knowledge and consent if they opt for a pension plan with a large pay-out and no survivor's benefits. Even so, continuing payments are seldom adequate to live on.

What about insurance? Like pay equity, it's slow to improve. The average settlement on a life insurance policy has risen from $7,000 twenty years ago to about $16,000. The average age at which a woman is widowed is still around fifty-six, so she has another nine years before she cuts in to OAS, for however much longer it's there in its present form.

"From birth to eighteen," said American entertainer Sophie Tucker, "a girl needs good parents. From eighteen to thirty-five, she needs good looks. From thirty-five to fifty-five, she needs a good personality. From fifty-five on, she needs good cash." We all need good cash.

Here's a summary of the possible sources of income for a widow, depending on her age:

- Canada Pension Plan – on earned income, at retirement
  – Widow's Allowance (see above)
- Family Allowance – for younger widows with minor children
- Old Age Security – for those sixty-five and over
- Guaranteed Income Supplement – for older citizens in greater need
- Registered Retired Savings Plan(s) – If you have one as well, your husband's can be rolled over into yours with no tax penalty; if you are past RRSP age, it can be rolled over into a RRIF (Registered Retirement Income Fund) or LIF (Life Income Fund). Your purpose is not to be hit with a large tax bill.
- Private pension plan
  – what's left for the survivor?
  – or her own, from work?
- Investments, if any
- Insurance settlement – Remember that lump sums of income can cost a lot in taxes.
- House
- Job.

The last three require further discussion; in fact, the last one requires another chapter.

Life insurance and its agents have been kicked around a lot over the years. Agents have been accused of backing the hearse up to the door; the industry itself has been criticized for using other people's money for inordinate gains. Perhaps in the past there was some truth to that, and yet in the past often the only thing that stood between a widow and complete ruin was an insurance settlement. My husband's mother reared her three children on an income of twenty-seven dollars a month from an insurance policy. Although there are other, more sophisticated means of creating a nest egg, a bulwark against the future, life insurance remains one of the easiest, most foolproof methods.

Even as I was rewriting this chapter, I heard of a man, fifty-six years old, a self-employed (no benefits) handyman and automotive repairman, who jacked up a car, didn't brace it, and was crushed to death when it fell on him. He had no insurance and no will. It still happens.

No matter the size of the claim you received, it's welcome money. As I've said, you can pay off the mortgage on the house, one of the best uses of a large sum of money at this point. You can set up a couple of GICs, as my lawyer did for me (I not knowing enough then to put up an umbrella in the rain), with the interest income staggered to give you something like a bimonthly living allowance – a good idea only when interest rates are high. Depending on your age you can set up a RRIF, LIF, or annuity to provide an income into your old age. Again, it depends on interest rates. You'll have to get information and advice on this.

As all the insurance claims are being settled, both private and group, be sure to double-check on everything that's coming to you. If your husband suffered a lengthy terminal illness, he/you may be eligible to receive a refund on premiums through a disability waiver clause, that is, if you didn't claim it before. You may have been too distraught or too busy to notice. Don't be afraid to ask questions. In the case of a company settlement, be sure to ask about your husband's pension fund, any accrued or vacation or sick pay, terminal pay allowances or death benefits, service recognition awards, unpaid commissions, credit union balance, whatever. You're a squirrel, gathering acorns for the long winter ahead.

As for your personal insurance for the future, your needs are very different, again depending on your age. If you're relatively young with dependent children and still working outside the home, you need income protection even more than you need life insurance. That means disability insurance. Younger women are far more likely to suffer disability than death, and if they have young children, disability is a fate worse than death. As for the future of your family, your best and cheapest bet is term insurance on your life. I took it out when my three older children were in university and my youngest, brain-damaged son was going through a horrible withdrawal. I wanted there to be enough money available to care for Matt in the event of my death so that the others' lives might not be too disrupted. Like any other financial tools, insurance can be fitted to your needs. Again, shop around, ask for help.

Most widows don't need life insurance unless they have either a dependent parent or a dependent adult child who needs their care. In this case, a joint and last survivor policy can be arranged. Other than that, you might want a small policy to pay for the last flurry: ambulance, funeral expenses, and so on. If you think your estate is large enough, these costs can be covered from a current cash account. Taxes being what they are, it would be wise not to die before you use up your own RRSP, because if the money goes into your estate, it is taxable and could eat up the capital. It's possible you won't care. If you do, you might want to take out a small policy to cover this expense. Your insurance agent can advise you.

I never met a life insurance agent who wasn't eager to help. Most agents call waitresses by their first names, coach Little League, join Rotary, and never litter. They really want to know how to help the bereaved and willingly sponsor educational programs for widows on both a small and large scale. These days, insurance agents and undertakers do more for the bereaved than ministers, priests, or rabbis, because people are more likely to bump into them. I note that funeral associations have begun to offer grief-counselling programs, especially valuable to ageing Boomers who have had few close encounters with death. War has not cut them off in their prime, or their friends; lower birth mortality and improved immunization have made the death of infants and children a rarer occurrence than ever before; and the increased longevity of Boomers' parents has been a bonus to their children, who have more grandparents than kids have ever had before. But all these factors have rendered the Boomer Generation less prepared to cope with the facts of death. The very idea of death, other than the make-believe, wholesale slaughter in movies, is alien. It's something that happens to other people. No one is prepared for it. (Were we ever?) This includes the younger widows among you, all in need of comfort and advice at a time when organized religion is losing its power to supply them.

As for the practical advice, I'll discuss financial planners in a minute, but in the meantime, do listen to what your insurance company, among others, offers. Some companies will even give you a copy of this book. That doesn't mean you have to accept everything they tell you. It won't hurt to gather all the information you can muster.

The Canadian Life and Health Insurance Association (CLHIA) is an umbrella organization servicing its member life insurance companies, providing information that is available to the general public on a single-copy basis. (Check "Resources" for an updated list of publications free for the asking.) CLHIA also has a toll-free hot line staffed by former life insurance agents (they don't die, they just go on hold) who are there to answer your questions about life insurance. The toll-free number is 1-800-268-8099.

Another valuable resource is your house, if you're fortunate enough to own one. It's probably your biggest investment and should be protected. I've said elsewhere and I say here: Do not move for at least a year if you can possibly help it. Enough has happened to you, and to your children, if they're still with you, without this further upheaval in your life. Live with the memories and the comfort of the last home you and your husband shared. You'll know when the time has come to move on, if it ever does. I have known lots of older widows who have remained in their home for the rest of their lives, not always a great solution, for several reasons.

It costs as much to heat one body as two, and a draughty old house may eat up fixed income faster than the slightly diminished food bills can compensate for. Maintenance is often difficult for shrinking dollars, ageing limbs, and dwindling energy to handle; too many empty rooms can be depressing and nerve-making; a house is hard to walk away from, even for a brief holiday, without arranging for its care. The sale of a large house may well cover the price of a modest apartment, with money left over for investment. Long before *old* old age sets in, a spry widow may get a new lease on life along with a lease on a condo with all services included.

Back to the grim present and younger widowed you. You must consider your house your biggest investment and you must look after it, that is, don't let it fall apart. Be meticulous about maintenance, painting, repairing, improving as required. Then when or if the time comes that you have to sell the house, its value will not have decreased.

By all means, use your insurance settlement to pay off your mortgage. Most policies have mortgage insurance, and I hope your husband opted for it. If not, use a lump of cash to pay off the house. It's still true that you may get a compassionate waiver of the penalty fee if you do this now. Timing is everything. A paid-up house is a bargaining chip for almost anything you need to do. For example, it's good collateral for a loan. A clear house gives you the best interest rate on a line of credit, a floating one pegged to the current rates, that is, if the rates are low. If the rates are high and you think they're going to go higher, then lock in your payment rate if you can.

Your house can also provide you with a source of income in later years, if need be. Reverse mortgages have become an important source of money to older house-holders who need more than they expected. Many older people have retired with what looked like a comfortable arrangement only to have lower interest rates and increasing expenses erode their income; it can be worse for one alone. It's possible to set up a reverse mortgage whereby the bank buys but does not take possession of the house, paying a monthly premium which sweetens the cash flow of the owner(s). The bad news is that if the house is paid for before the owner dies, she no longer has a roof over her head, a risk that must be considered.

A granny mortgage, so-called because it usually involves a widowed mother, is an arrangement whereby a son or daughter of the granny buys a house and asks her to hold the mortgage. The younger couple pay her, usually at an attractive rate of interest – to them. In return, she usually lives rent-free in the house with them, preferably (for both sides) in an apartment or separate quarters of her own. As more people are living longer, these and other solutions to income and living problems will become more and more common.

We're talking future here, long-range stuff. In the meantime, you are still wondering how you're going to get through tomorrow, let alone next year. Quite apart from the pain, that emotional blood bath you are staggering through, you are, quite simply, scared. Let's hope you aren't as helpless and hopelessly uninformed as I was, but even if you aren't, there are two kinds of paralysis you have to deal with before you can make dollars and sense of your life.

The first is emotional: grief is compounded by fear, making it almost impossible at times for you to make a decision, let alone a move. In an odd way, you can be grateful for the financial pressure. It forces you to do something. I've said so often that it's like an old refrain: You have to have a reason to get out of bed in the morning. Having to earn a living is a very good reason.

I am told that the AAs have a saying, "Move a muscle and the mind will follow." I'm sure this maxim applies to grief, too. The pain of bereavement can be addictive: at least you're still feeling something and that's better than being numb, staring at the wall unable to move. But if you have to move, that is, if you have to get up and go to work in order to pay the rent or the taxes, if you have to balance a brand-new budget, then your muscle and your mind and soon, maybe, even your raw feelings will follow.

About that budget: it's time to draw one up. This is why I began with a summary of your possible sources of income. Write down the ones that apply to you and the figures that go with them, in other words, analyse your net income. Now do a rough assessment of your expenditures. I say rough because your life has changed, more than you realize at first. Husbands, bless them, are not only time-consuming, they're also expensive. Some of your expenses will automatically plummet in this sad absence of the person it was the most fun to be extravagant with. Some costs, however, are not only no fun, they're also fixed, like hydro, phone, rent or mortgage payments, taxes, and so on. Nevertheless, write them down, and then compare your outgo with your income, see where you're at.

Don't forget to allow for saving. Unless you're already in your eighties, you're going to have to save enough for creature comforts in the end zone. I'll tell you the best item to write into your new budget. Lynne MacFarlane and I said it in our money book and we keep on saying it at every opportunity:

*Save 10 per cent of your income.*

The second part of this imperative is equally important:

*Pay yourself first.*

Treat this expense like your other regular bills and make it your first priority. The simplest, most painless way of doing this is to estimate your gross annual income, figure out what 10 per cent of that is monthly, and arrange for a regular withdrawal from your chequing account. Withdrawal to where? Have the amount deposited into a mutual fund or a Canada Savings Bond account or an ongoing RRSP, although I would prefer that your 10 per cent be over and above your RRSP savings. If you think that's too heavy to start, build up to it. You'll find that when the money isn't there, you won't spend it. I know that sounds terribly simplistic, but money is.

The other paralysing factor you have to deal with is peculiar to women, the old Cinderella syndrome that Constance Dowling describes in her 1981 book *The Cinderella Complex*, still in print. It seems to be terribly true that the minute a prince heaves into view, a woman – even a tough, strong, independent one who's been earning her own living for years and who has gone on working after her marriage – dwindles into a wife. I deplored my own incompetence and lack of

54

knowledge about money and the business world, blaming the protected state of my role as housewife and my own airheadedness, but I found I was not alone, not then and not now. As Dowling writes, "The amount of self-confidence women have is in inverse proportion to the performance level of their partners. Remarkably, *the higher the partner's performance, the less likely the woman is to attribute competence to herself.*" (her emphasis)

Recently I hosted and helped to produce a thirteen-part television series about women and money. Most of the people involved in the show were women, seven high-powered, intelligent career women who you would expect to have a firm grasp of their finances. Until I started nagging, not one of them was saving 10 per cent of her income. Only one had recently updated her will – and I did, too, after I interviewed a lawyer for one of the shows. If you don't have a will or haven't updated it within the last three years, waste no time. While you're at it, arrange with your lawyer for a power of attorney, the agreement to be deposited with her rather than with your children, and arrange also for a separate power of personal care, which may be left with one of your children (or a caregiver). My associates had done nothing about these documents either.

Nor were they using their RRSP allowance to its fullest extent. (Each year, millions of eligible RRSP dollars go unspent that might be giving its owners a tax shelter as well as guaranteeing a future nest egg.) No one belonged to an investment club until I interviewed a group of women who belonged to one. Most of my cohorts were overdrawn on their credit cards, which demand the worst terms you can get on a loan. This was standard behaviour from vital, contemporary business-women, all but one of them single. So I was not unique in my former ignorance; in fact, I think I'm unique now because I know a lot more than I did.

I had a separate bank account and I knew how to write a cheque. I have met many women since who do not possess this basic skill. I could drive a car, a little shaky on parallel parking, but I knew my licence number. Then I met a woman who didn't know where the brights were because her husband wouldn't let her drive at night. When I told that story, another woman came up to tell me that she didn't know a car needed oil! I watched a friend I was visiting in Winnipeg go out to discover her car was dead and come in to call her husband rather than the service station. When I announced during another talk that I had just bought my first car all by myself, and arranged my first bank loan, my audience cheered. As well they should, because I had begun to exist as a financial entity.

You must know that you do not exist in the world of finance – that is, you do not have a credit rating, therefore you are invisible – until you have actually gone into debt and paid it off. (You can find out what your credit rating is by phoning the Credit Bureau nearest you and asking.) As part of your clean-up job, be sure to change the name on any credit cards you hold and make sure the company realizes that you are no longer the second holder of the card. You're it. Some companies will send you an application form and begin again; that's fine. Go for it. The easiest way to get credit is to have a good credit rating. You never know when you may need approval. Most recently I arranged my first car lease, having figured out that for tax purposes it's better to lease a car in January (or buy in December) and that as a self-employed person I get a good tax credit for leasing. I keep learning something new all the time, not only learning, but doing something about it. Anyway, I had no trouble getting approval from the leasing company because I have a good credit rating. I pay, therefore I am.

By the way, pay attention to the goodies provided in the car lease or purchase agreement. You may be entitled to roadside assistance, in which case you can forget about joining an automobile club. On the other hand, lots of people enjoy both; don't forget those neat little maps and routes CAA offers as part of the membership privileges.

I'd like to think that if Cinderella were alive today, she'd start a cottage industry, making glass ornaments much in demand at exclusive gift shops, especially those cunning little slippers. She would also arrange a good marriage contract with the Prince, keeping control of the business she brought into the union. I'm not being all that facetious, I'm just trying to cheer you up. You may feel helpless, but you're not. Even if you are – helpless not stupid, only ignorant – help is available. You must have noticed that every women's magazine going has a money column now; financial advice is more important than cake recipes and make-up diagrams these days. Books about money abound: the romance of mutual funds, the thrill of the stock market, the mystery of financial planning, all are yours for the reading. You can read a book, but you can also take a course. You can join an investment club and dip your toe into the stock market. You can also engage a financial planner.

It used to be that only rich people hired a financial planner, people who possessed storied millions to invest and shelter. Now a humble, low-salaried employee can ask (and pay for) advice. The rate per hour varies, from $150 to $250 for an evaluation of your situation and some recommendations for a plan of action. Remember TNSTAFL: There's No Such Thing As a Free Lunch. However, a "free" assessment is available from planners associated with a company or companies (plural means the planner is a broker) whose products they sell. They throw in the evaluation and take a percentage of your investments instead. For this fee, you as client are entitled to a once- or twice-a-year check-up to chart your progress and receive further advice. The service is quite valuable, depending on how conscientious the guru is.

The qualifications of financial planners read like alphabet soup, that is, the initials after their names indicating their degrees of expertise. Make it your business to find out what those letters mean. Then shop around. You're good at that.

Income, outgo, the little numbers on the page add up to a lifestyle, perhaps very different from the one you were used to. That was then, this is now. You haven't lost your wits, though at times it may feel like it. Here are some money-saving tips I have culled from the last edition together with a few new angles I've picked up. I hope they will make you feel both more human and more competent as you keep on coping day by day by day.

1. Use credit cards like cash and pay off your account in full every month. If something comes up and you can't make the full payment, use overdraft protection or a line of credit from your bank instead of paying the card company's outrageous interest rate. Also, don't borrow cash on a credit card (as people sometimes do when travelling) because you pay interest on it immediately.

2. Use your float. Notice when your account closes each month. You usually have about ten days to two weeks to pay. If you save a major purchase until after the monthly close, you have six weeks to pay for it (making sure that you can pay the entire bill when it arrives). If you have a daily interest account, it means you get the benefit of your money a little longer.

3. Leave your credit card(s) at home one week a month. You'd be surprised how much money you save. It's estimated that impulse purchases made with the

sleight of hand a card makes so easy add 10 per cent to your bill. One December I lost my wallet (actually, it had fallen under the seat of the car) and after I cancelled everything I had to go through the month before Christmas operating on cash. Not only did I spend less, I ended up in January without huge bills to pay. I learned something else then and did something about it: I cancelled all my cards but one. Let one company do your bookkeeping for you and pay one bill; it's simpler. I do have a friend in a volatile business, however, self-employed, who says he got through a very lean time by juggling several credit cards, paying off his minimum on each, and letting the companies carry him until he was in an earning position again. Maybe men have more nerve than women; I couldn't do that.

4. If you get a raise or a gift or a bonus, any unexpected income, don't spend it. Put it into your Money Market Fund ready to be moved into a mutual fund (you'll have this all set up after you meet with your financial planner). If it's big enough, you can take out a ninety-day note or a term deposit. You'll have to compare interest rates with dividends and decide which gives you the better return.

On the other hand, I must admit that twice now when this has happened to me, I blew it all on a trip. The first time I used a large, totally unexpected fee to pay for a photographic safari to Kenya, and I don't even take pictures. The second time, more recently, a pleasant and also unexpected royalty arrived in time to pay for a frivolous week in Paris at the end of an intensive work period.

I said to my daughter Kate, "I've decided I won't mind when I'm ninety and living in a hovel." And she said, "I'll remind you."

I'm not recommending constant treats beyond your means, but I have always maintained that you have to sniff the flowers on your way by.

5. If you have a bank loan or car, furniture or mort-gage payments that eventually get paid off, don't stop making the payments. Make them to yourself, another way of squirrelling away more than the 10 per cent of your income you're already saving.

6. Do make sure your bank loan or mortgage is insured; that way, the debt is automatically paid in the event of your death.

7. Don't carry as much cash as you did. See how little you can get along with, but don't be chintzy. Look on it as a way to lose weight and skip the doughnut with your coffee.

8. Shop for groceries when you're not hungry. Impulses account for 25 per cent of expenditures in a supermarket (more for men). Do you really need a can of artichoke hearts? Make a shopping list and stick to it.

9. That means making a menu plan for the week. A plan saves not only money but time. I always make mine with the refrigerator door open, checking the contents to see what has to be used up. Long ago I wrote a cookbook about leftovers; most recently I have written a cookbook for singles, combining my expertise with leftovers with what I have learned cooking for one. It really is a challenge.

10. I hate coupons. I recommend using them, but if you're like me, you leave them in your wallet until you check the expiry dates and throw them away with a clear conscience.

11. On the other hand, keep track of and use your air miles on various frequent-flyer programs. (I guess I just like big savings.)

12. Since I moved out of the city I have become a catalogue shopper, but I understand that city dwellers, too, have become addicted to shopping by mail (or Internet or Home Shopping). I enjoy browsing and I circle the things I like. Then I make a list of them and see

what they add up to, decide what I need as opposed to what I want and can afford. Sometimes I go all the way to filling out the order form and then – toss it into the fire. My little aphorism, so elementary it sounds simplistic, is this: *The best way to save money is not to spend it.*

13. Recycle things. Of course you have a Blue Box and haul out your newspapers and bottles and tin cans, but how are you on paper? Do you reuse big envelopes? Write your grocery lists on the back of used paper? Cut the pretty pictures from the front of Christmas and other cards either to give to craft projects at your local school or day care or to use yourself next year as enclosure cards?

14. Some people carry their saving graces much further. Plastic milk bags, rinsed out and dried, make wonderful flat, protective envelopes for snapshots or small items. I know women, older than I, who never buy wax paper or sandwich bags because they save the liners from cereal boxes and the bags from bread. I use my plastic grocery bags for garbage and never buy white plastic ones. It's called a depression mentality. (I was two.)

15. Walk to do a small errand rather than take the car – good for you, too. You'll do the planet a favour as well as yourself if you think before you squander your/our resources.

It pays to be resourceful.

Though you may have suffered a drastic change in your income, you will find that your wants and needs have dwindled as well. While your family, safety, security, food, and shelter are paramount, fun and games and self-indulgence come far down on your list. Your life is going to be different, no doubt about that. With or without a lot of money, it's going to be different; it already is. As soon as you feel up to it, take stock of your future, being aware as you never were before of how quickly things can change and of how much is beyond your control.

I'll summarize for you what I consider to be your basic moves, the first being *don't make a move*. I know I've said that before, several times. You may think you're sane but you're not. Any major move you make concerning your house, your investments, or your lifestyle, no matter how rational you think it is, is not. It's merely rash. Give yourself time for the smoke and your head to clear. Sit tight. Hold still. Stay there. You have a lot to learn before you make a reasoned decision. Wait at least six months; a year is better, if you can afford it.

While you're waiting, *stay involved*. Keep learning. Sitting there doesn't mean doing nothing. In fact, you'll probably be busier than you have ever been as you acquaint yourself with the business of your life. Even if you knew what you were doing before (as I did not), it's not the same without your closest friend and companion to confide in. So the first thing you might want to do is look around and *find someone to consult*. This can be tricky. Your children, even grown-up ones, don't always understand or know (or care) what's best for you.

I know one widow, well-off, who decided after a suitable length of time that she wanted to do some serious travelling. Her adult son did his best to dissuade her. He advised her instead to invest her money wisely. His main reason, which he didn't say out loud to her, was that he wanted her to keep her money intact for himself. If you're as materially fortunate as that woman, pay heed to the bumper sticker "I'm spending my children's inheritance" and go ahead and enjoy.

Your husband's best friend may be a great golfer and salt of the earth, but he may not be the wisest financial adviser you can find. The same goes for your family lawyer. Therefore, *be very picky about the brains you pick*. Free but untutored advice may cost you more in the long run than professional counselling. At the same time, once you have found a financial planner who suits you and who understands your needs, *don't hand over your brains along with your money*. It doesn't hurt to consult a few people – friends, family, teacup reader (I'm joking), your accountant. Don't consult with too many and don't play yes-but. Once you have carefully weighed your alternatives, make a decision and live with it. Today is not forever. Nobody knows that better than you do. I've already cautioned you to shop around for a financial planner. Do I need to warn you about the new man (if any) in your life? Trust takes time to build and must be proven. I guess the key to any choice you make is to make sure that anyone who advises you is not putting his or her welfare ahead of yours.

Incidentally, if you decide to marry again, you should seriously consider a marriage contract, being sure to retain what you brought into the second marriage for your own family (if that's what you want). This advice applies equally to widowers, if not more so. Everyone should beware of sweet talkers and schemes that are too good to be true, because they usually are.

Yes, Virginia, there is life after bereavement, and while it may not be as much fun, it need not be desperate. Given some thought, juggling, and a little help, you'll manage. Now that you've learned how to count, be sure to count your blessings.

# 5

# Moving on

*How quickly, in one instant, years of happy life become only memories!*

*Pearl Buck*

There is a phrase engineers use to describe the position of an object when it stops moving. It is called the "angle of repose." Your husband has reached his angle of repose but you haven't. You haven't stopped moving yet. As long as we live we keep on changing.

The first autumn after Bill died, I went ahead as usual and made jams, jellies, pickles, etc. I don't have a second hand on my watch or my kitchen clock. I always used to use my husband to time my jelly-stirring (or count "a-thousand-and-one-"). So when I had to stir my jelly that first fall, I ran upstairs and got his watch to help me out. It was the first time I had looked at it. The date had changed – it stopped 12 hours after he died.

I can stand that, I thought. I can stand that. And I can. I can stand anything. I didn't know that before. You can, too.

I haven't made jelly since, or pickles, but for other

reasons than you might suspect. First, my family did not use up the supplies within the year as they did before. Second, I lost my interest in cooking. Third, I became too busy doing other things. Fourth, there was no storage space in my new home for preserves. You see, I moved.

Divorce, quipped a recent divorcée, is learning how to change your own lightbulbs. That applies to widowhood, too. I know there are lots of married women who change the lightbulbs, and take out the garbage, too, but it is a comforting knowledge that there is another, usually taller, person in the house who can change a ceiling bulb or get something down from the top shelf in the kitchen without standing on a stepstool.

There are men who are not handy around the house: my father wasn't; my husband was only slightly better; my son John is a whiz. One out of three isn't bad. It's a stereotype that says men have to be good at fixing toaster plugs and unstopping clogged toilets while women sew on the buttons and make the porridge. If I lose a button I might as well throw the garment away. I'm three years behind in my mending.

But when one becomes a widow, suddenly the home chores become terribly important. Who's going to do them? Who's going to applaud you when you do them? It's not only that it's work you have to do yourself, it's also that there's no zest in doing it. Why bother? Do you want to put up Christmas lights this year? Do you need to put bedding plants in? Does the fence really need painting?

A lot of the inertia of grief spills over into the process of living. C.S. Lewis commented on it in his book *A Grief Observed*: "No one," he wrote, "ever told me about the laziness of grief. Except at my job – where the machine seems to run on much as usual – I loathe the slightest effort. . . . It's easy to see why the lonely become untidy."

It's not only the grass-mowing, the snow-shovelling,

the broken windows, garbage, leaky faucets and eaves-troughs, sticking doors, and burnt-out light bulbs. Even more oppressive in the single-handed care and upkeep of a home are the major repairs and maintenance. It's making a decision, getting the thing done, and paying the bill – all for something you don't really care about as much anymore. Like every other problem widows face, it looms large because you're facing it alone. And there's no satisfaction in it when you do tackle a job, because who notices? Who cares?

If you think I'm giving you an argument for not owning a house, you're not completely right. Certainly I am not advising you to rush away from it. Running a house by yourself is only one more of the many challenges you face as a single person. It can be done. And there are rewards.

I have said elsewhere that you should not make any major decision – and moving would be a major one – hastily. Sit tight for at least a year, if you can, after your husband's death, while you take stock and measure your own abilities and attitudes. But don't let the house go to seed while you sit there. In the same way, you have been urged by your friends (haven't you?) not to "let yourself go," you mustn't neglect the maintenance of your home. Your house is probably your biggest single investment. Don't be afraid to spend some money on it. Take care of it. Then when you do decide to move, you'll get your money out of it.

Wonderful changes have taken place which may make your tasks easier. There are courses available all over the country for women to learn how to carpenter, do electrical repairs, car maintenance, upholstery, etc., and women are taking them and learning how to cope, to their great satisfaction. I know a single woman who does all her own remodelling. If there is something she doesn't know how to do, she takes a course on the subject and learns. Her home is a showcase, an apartment in a beautiful old house, and she has done all the refinishing, carpentry, papering, painting, and electrical installations herself. A former neighbour of mine, married, took a woodworking course and built a magnificent pool table for her husband and sons. It is a work of art. The only things she bought ready-made were the balls and the cues. Next she panelled the rec room. And there are women to whom gardening is no chore, as it is to me, who find great satisfaction in keeping their gardens glowing and beautiful. And then there are others like me who would rather have everything done for them. I'll stand by the sidelines and cheer and provide sandwiches and coffee and first aid, if necessary, for the workers. I was fortunate that my son John was handy around the house. At fourteen he took over the house, pool, and yard maintenance and I never had cause for complaint. But I realized that first summer when he went away to camp how dependent I was on him. I couldn't have done it by myself, nor did I want to.

One of the clichés of widowhood is the clingy little neighbourhood widow who needs help from her neighbours' husbands. There were times, I'll admit, when I found that help necessary. I tried to avoid criticism by inviting both husband and wife over for drinks or coffee and a snack while I explained my problem. That way I got some company and some free help, and the wife was assured that I had no designs on her husband outside of his plumbing or financial skills or whatever. There really are problems you encounter that men can solve more easily, but you do have to be careful how you go about asking them to solve them. Their wives resent it, and men often get the idea that that isn't the only problem you have that needs a man's touch.

But that's something else again. The point I am trying to make is that, ept or not, it is possible for you to go on living where you have been living and to cope by yourself. The libraries are full of how-to books, and some of them are written especially for women.

Staying on in the last home you and your husband shared together has its own kind of comfort. The pictures on the walls were probably discussed and hung by both of you in consultation; all the decorating decisions surrounding you were probably joint ones. A presence lingers that is sustaining. On the other hand, when and if the time comes to move, that can be good, too. As one widow said, "Moving is like closing the wound; you're healed and you move on." Take your time, though. Think about it. No rush.

I'm afraid we rushed my mother when my father died. I didn't know as much then as I do now. We thought the reasons were good and valid, but I can see now she should have had more time. Moving is a traumatic experience and should not follow too hard on the heels of the death of one's mate. The house still retains echoes and memories which are comforting. Your mind resists change. Any decision you make is apt to be woolly-headed and unreasonable. And the inertia of the body makes one incapable of the large amounts of energy required for moving.

On the other hand, it often happens now that a woman can be stranded by the death of her husband in a city that is strange to her. I myself had lived in Stratford only five years when Bill died. The friends we had made were obviously not lifelong friends. That can make a big difference in terms of long-term support and concern. If you find yourself in a strange community, perhaps in spite of my admonitions not to move too quickly or hastily, the best thing would be to move back to your hometown. I know two widows who did just that, both within a month of their husbands' deaths, and it was the right thing for them to do. Both of them have since remarried, by the way. I don't know if there's a moral to that story or not.

My reasons for moving were as complex as yours might be. I was tired of taking care of the house all by myself. I was tired of living in a small city, one which I discovered did not adapt easily to singles in its midst. I was tired of living in a ghetto of women, and, particularly, of widows. I felt things would be different in a larger city, and they have been. But most of all, I was tired of driving on Highway 401 to Toronto. I like driving, but not in blizzards or sleet or ice storms. And on the highway as nowhere else I was aware of the responsibility I had to take very good care of my children's only parent.

"Drive carefully," John would say as I left the house, "I don't want to live with someone else."

I was spending too much time on the highway because all my work was in Toronto. I knew I could increase my income if I moved because I would be where the work was. Driving time is unproductive time. Incidentally, a move for financial reasons such as mine earns a tax credit.

I didn't know many widows my age but the ones I did know were affected by my decision. One of them also sold her house and moved out of town, as I did. Another put her house on the market, quit her job, took a course, and found a better job. Another stayed where she was but made envious noises and became more dissatisfied with her life. She needed another catalyst.

For many different reasons, a widow may find that the home she maintained when she was her husband's wife no longer suits her needs. It may be too expensive, too much trouble to keep up, too large as the family keeps shrinking, too empty when the widow is left alone. If enough time has passed that the reasons for moving are based on common sense and logic and not on some emotional gut reaction, then by all means move.

A move for a widow usually means a reduction in space. Whether you move from one house or apartment to another, or from a house to an apartment, the new space is usually smaller than the old space – that's part of the reason for moving, isn't it? That means getting rid of a lot of the stuff in the present space in order to fit into the new, smaller space. It means, finally, taking stock of your past, your marriage, and your possessions. And it means finding out more things about yourself. Such as, how important are possessions to you? How important is space? How much space? A garden? Neighbours? Memories? Habits?

Take your time. Consider it the biggest spring (or fall) cleaning you've ever undertaken. Go over everything. Find out what your children want, and give it to them or save it for them. Have a garage sale. Sell things or give them away, but get rid of them.

Strange reactions happen, but welcome them. This is another purge and it's valuable. I found I was reliving a future that was no longer going to occur. Things I had put away for our old age together I no longer needed, so they went out. My scenario is different; I need different props. It was not only my past I was clearing, it was also my future, and that's valuable, if somewhat painful.

We end up owning many things not by choice but by accident, because we needed something in a hurry, because someone else thought we needed something and gave it to us, because it was on sale, because it fit a room or a specific purpose at the time. How seldom it is given to anyone to choose again, or if not to choose, at least to discriminate! What you finally end up with, when you move as a widow, is what you choose to keep. As your lifestyle changes, so do your needs. New possessions gradually reveal the changes in you. You are becoming a different person.

We live in such a materialistic age; we all accumulate things like squirrels. I can't tell you what a pleasure it was to begin to divest myself of some of my possessions. I felt like Diogenes with his bowl. Remember the story of the Greek philosopher who owned nothing but a bowl in which he collected the food he begged to keep himself alive? One day he tripped and broke his bowl and he said, "At last! I'm free!" I still own too much, but I own a lot less than I did. It's nice to be lighter and freer than I was.

I had the biggest garage sale in the world, and that was a revelation in itself. I heartily recommend garage sales. People will buy anything if it's on sale, and I mean anything. There is a little paperback with complete advice on such sales, and most women's magazines have tips on them every spring. All you have to do is go to one or two and learn how for yourself. I sold tired Christmas wrap and decorations and lights, broken hockey sticks, boxes of torn sheets, threadbare towels and rags (useful for painters and mechanics, I found), toys and clothes and ornaments and glasses, old dolls with the eyes blunk out, tablecloths and placemats and utensils, clothes, appliances, furniture, carpets and lawn chairs, and my neighbour's new broom that she swept my garage floor with and left leaning against a wall. I sold my past and parts of my future that no longer existed. I'm afraid I sold some of my children's past and future, too, and I feel sorry about that.

Storage in my parents' home remained available to me until long after I was married. I didn't fully claim all my possessions until we were living in our third home. I'm sorry I couldn't grant that kind of carefree space to my children. Others suffer that deprivation, though, whose moves are caused by reasons other than straitened circumstances following a death in the family. Army "brats," families in the diplomatic service, people who must move where the work is, all must travel light. Posterity may wish for the kind of mementoes earlier generations stored in dusty attics and mildewed basements, but not many people have that kind of space any more.

Moving is harder on the children who are at home. I had hoped to spare them the move at least until John was finished high school, but as I became more and more busy in Toronto and unhappy in Stratford, I realized that two years out of my life at my age were more important than two years out of his life at his age, so I didn't wait. It is hard on kids to move in their teens, late in their high school years. They have no time to form new allegiances. They become aliens when it is desperately important for them to belong. I know that, and I'm sorry, and it's something you should consider if it applies. But John found a compensation in the fact that I was nicer to live with and around a lot more (instead of on the highway) once we'd moved. There are times you have to make the decision for yourself, and let the others fall into line with you.

It's a case of weighing the advantages and disadvantages. There are times when you have to cut your losses and run. You do it materially when you move. You have to take a beating on some of the things you're selling off, as you might expect. You can't get much for second-hand furniture. You'll just have to consider the difference between what you paid originally and what you finally received for it as rent for the use of it. You can't take it with you – there's no room. So move on without it.

And that's what you have to do emotionally, too. You can't sit down and wither in the past. You can't wait out a future that doesn't exist. Take your memories with you, by all means, but move on.

# 6

# The working widow

*Those who do not complain are never pitied.*

*Jane Austen*

As long as men keep on acting like grasshoppers and women like Cinderella, widows (and divorcées) are going to have a lean time. Even so, they're better off than they used to be. In the Middle Ages, they were burned or drowned as witches. That doesn't happen any more. The percentage of them (i.e., single women over sixty-five) living below Low Income Cut-Off (the poverty line) has gone down in my widowed memory from 65 per cent to just under 40 per cent. Widows' CPP payments have increased – for however long that may last – mainly because some of them have worked outside the home and earned some pension money of their own; some of them, too, have learned something about finance and claim some income from investments. It's a beginning.

In the meantime, more women are living longer and more of them are living alone. Statistics Canada's analyses don't give me the figures I want for the number of widows in the country today (according to the 1981 census there were over a million); instead, I'm forced to juggle the numbers of single and lone-parent women and try to draw some conclusions. Women make up slightly more than half of all people living in Canada (1991 census); they represent 58 per cent of all people aged sixty-five and older – still outliving men, you see. Over 80 per cent of single-parent families were headed by women in 1991; 39 per cent of all women sixty-five and older lived alone, 11 per cent with other relatives, and 2 per cent with unrelated people. What I can't find is the ratio of widowed to divorced women, but I know that it has almost reversed in the last two decades, being more heavily weighted now on the side of the divorced.

Wage inequity continues for women of all ages. The gap seemed to be closing steadily during the early eighties, but it has levelled off in the nineties to about 70 per cent of men's wages, the closest approximation for full-time employment. The key phrase is full-time. In 1994, 69 per cent of all part-time workers in Canada were female. That figure has held steady over two decades, although a 1994 survey indicated that at least 34 per cent of female part-time workers would prefer full-time work but couldn't find it. In the meantime, unemployment figures in Canada have remained high in the nineties so that both higher wages and full-time work remain elusive. The bad news for you is: even if it hasn't happened yet, widowhood may take away your membership in the middle class.

I've already commented on the small amount of money the average death claim settles on the widow of an insured man and women's limited pension opportunities in general. In the past, widows have participated in the work force less than others, because many of them were older and had already reached their retirement years. However, with fixed incomes, lower interest rates, and inadequate pensions balancing more and more poorly against ever-variable inflation, even older widows find themselves attempting to increase their incomes through full or part-time work – not as easy to find as it used to be. Of those women bereaved at a younger age, that is, under retirement age, many of them have already been working outside the home, but it's a shock to find themselves dependent on the second income, usually much smaller than the first one, the husband's. Those not already working must go to work, perhaps after a gap of some fifteen to twenty-five years; those who are working must enhance their incomes. All of them need to develop competitive, marketable skills. In short, most widows need good jobs.

Trained or not, if a widow needs more money than she has coming in, she must find a means of supplementing – or creating – her income. The question is what will she do? There are as many answers to that as there are people, and both are a constant source of surprise. The more I see, and the more stories people tell me, the more certain I am that the best solution is to see a need and fill it; that is, make up your own job. Past a certain age, it may be the only way you'll get one.

I met a widow recently who told me she began to cook a hot lunch – for a fee – at her office every day, using the boardroom kitchen. It turned into a full-time job as her clientele increased. She had to study recipes, plan her menus, do her marketing, submit her expenses, balance her books, and, of course, keep cooking. But that's a good example of meeting a need that hadn't been met, and thereby creating a job. I know another widow who indulged a lifelong love of dolls by starting a dolls' hospital. Her painstaking, loving work is much in demand. Another widow was instrumental in starting a widows' counselling service through a local Y; she went to a community college to take the necessary courses and is now helping to run the service (for divorced persons as well) on a continuing, paid basis. My mother-in-law in her day took in a boarder to make ends meet. Half my baby-sitters when my children were small were older widows who turned their experience with children and their abiding interest in people into a service that is always in demand. What a widow does depends on her training, her age, her children, and her opportunities.

Women have generally tended to go into six or seven different occupations outside the home: waitressing, clerking, selling, all the low-paying services, plus teaching and nursing, which pay a little better but don't offer much chance of advancement. What women have to do now is break out of the mould and develop expertise in non-traditional areas. Of course, the future lies in computer-related skills, the more technical the better paying. If a woman is going to function as head of a household, she needs a decent wage, not merely a supplementary income. Play this need against the unemployment rates and similar needs of men, and we have a problem.

I am more and more convinced that people are going to have to create their own jobs. Our governments have demonstrated that they can't keep up with the demand. The world has changed unimaginably in my lifetime as it has, and will, in yours. At the turn of the century, an heiress thought that her fortune was secure because all her money was soundly invested in a stove-blacking company. After all, people were always going to need their wood-burning stoves well cleaned and blacked, weren't they? No, but by the end of the century, wood-burning stoves are coming back into fashion as an alternative source of heat as the supply of fossil fuels shrinks and hydro-electric power rises in cost. Ecologically minded citizens, wary of polluting the air with wood smoke, are working at developing cleaner-burning wood stoves. The father of American writer Henry David Thoreau had a lead-pencil factory, surely a safe and never-failing source of income; there would always be a need for pencils, wouldn't there? No, but a group of Luddites has formed a Lead Pencil Club, trying to make people think more slowly and carefully. Thomas Edison predicted that the electric light would render candles a luxury and not a necessity, and when you look at the price of candles in fancy candle and craft shops, you know he was right. I remember thinking as a teenager that some day I would like to be rich enough to have my own private screening room so that I could watch movies I liked over and over again. I'm not rich, but I can do that now with my very own VCR and rented or purchased videos.

The point of this digression is that none of us could have imagined the new jobs that accompany new discoveries. Recycling is becoming a boom industry; people are already inventing new uses for old material, such as houses and roads built of used tires and key chains and binders made of discarded computer chip boards. You might be the one to see a new need where a vacancy exists, such as the woman who created Renta Yentl, a service organization doing the jobs that stay-at-home mothers used to do, for a fee.

That's a need to note, several needs, in fact – all the myriad tasks that homemakers used to perform are no longer being done because no one's home. So now there are professional plant-waterers and pet-walkers and birthday-party caterers. The trick is to spot a need and fill it, capitalizing on skills you already possess. Or not. Break your pencil and go for computer training!

I went to work, of course, writing as I had all my life, but finally for money. I never stop analysing writing markets and ideas and having to come up with new ones. You may not want to write, but you can come up with new ideas.

What you need now is breakthrough thinking. Just because you've never done something before is no reason why you can't now. We're all mothers of invention when it comes to necessity. When people ask me how I can write so much, I answer with Samuel Johnson's line: "Depend upon it, sir: knowing you're going to be hanged in a fortnight concentrates the mind wonderfully." You, too, will find your mind concentrates wonderfully when there is a gun pointed at your head. The gun, of course, is the need for money.

That's Number One: need. Number Two is the job. Where is it? What you have to do is put together your need with the right job and you'll find what you're looking for: relief from anxiety, a decent salary, and self-respect. You may have to change your ideas about the kind of job you thought you wanted, that's all.

Even if you have specific skills, you may need brushing up – a refresher course in bookkeeping or shorthand, or transcribing from a tape, and some computer training to teach your typing fingers how to handle a mouse. Some fields have changed so much that your refresher course might well take one or two years at a community college. The help is available.

If further training is necessary before a suitable job can be found, there are more resources available now than there ever have been. If a woman already holds a high school diploma she can take further courses at most colleges across Canada. Information and catalogues are available from the universities. Most universities now allow credits for "life experience" to mature students; people past a certain age (usually the early twenties) are allowed to register as mature students and take courses. Ask about these when you write for catalogues and other information. Enquire, too, about bursaries, scholarships, and student loan plans.

All right, you've done your personal inventory. You are trained and ready and you know what you want to do. Now you can take a look at the job. You have to consider the built-in costs. If child-care is necessary, that is a major expense. There are insufficient spaces in day-care centres for all the children who require care; in-home care continues to be a solution for a lot of working mothers. Often, in the case of a pre-school child, a relative or close friend or neighbour is the only available answer. Make it a financial arrangement if you can. It lasts longer, and there are tax credits.

There is also a difficult twilight zone in children's ages that presents a different problem and requires a different solution. What about the children who are of school age, fairly competent, but still too young to make their own lunch or not quite responsible enough to be at loose ends after school until someone comes home? School lunches, or again a reliable neighbour (on a paid basis to guarantee continuity), and after-school programs are all necessities in this case.

My younger son was signed up term after term for after-school programs for which I was deeply grateful. What was more, the school allowed single parents and working mothers to sign up first, showing great understanding of our pressures. Matthew ended up knowing more about macramé, cooking, ceramics, creative dance, floor hockey, and woodworking than he cared to, but I knew he was constructively occupied until I got home.

There are other expenses. You may need a car, or if you have one, you may use it more, to transport your child to and from day care. How far do you have to travel to get to the job? Can you afford the transportation costs? And the time it takes you to get to and from your work? You will have to spend more on clothes, on lunches (brown bag it!), on faster-cooking, more expensive food. Your lifestyle changes again when you take a full-time job; make sure it is a change for the better, one that you will welcome for the challenge and stimulus and not one that is going to drag you down and make you tired and more discouraged than ever.

If you take a full-time job, chances are you will have some sort of company or group policy, and chances are equally good that there is a disability clause in it. Check it out. It could be worse, at this stage of your life, if you were disabled and unable to work than if you were dead, for all practical purposes. Child support continues to be necessary no matter where you are, so be sure to find out about this.

If you're working full-time, you will automatically be part of the Canada Pension Plan. Even part-time workers, or self-employed ones like myself, participate in CPP or QPP (Quebec Pension Plan); you do it at income-tax time, and it's quite painless. However, you must sweeten your future by setting up a Registered Retirement Savings Plan for yourself.

It is likely, once you start working, that you will continue to do so until retirement age. This is your new vocation, beyond that of wife and mother. Take a look at your long-term goals and be sure you're going where you want to go. If you don't have any goals, maybe you should think about that, too. You're alone now. You're you. What are you? And where are you going? What do you want? If you think I'm asking tough questions, you're right. I've been asking myself the same ones.

I wrote these questions in the fall of 1977 when this book was first published. At the same time, I had a new play produced, a children's play called *The Old Woman and the Pedlar*, based on the nursery rhyme about an old woman who is sleeping by the side of the road when a pedlar comes along and cuts her petticoats all round about.

"Lawk-a-mercy me," she says when she wakes up. "This is none of I," and she sets about trying to discover who she is if she is not herself. The whole play is a quest. The old woman encounters different people on the road and asks for their help, to no avail. Finally, in despair, she gives up, saying that she's lost all hope.

With that, a sweet, adenoidal games-mistress type of creature comes on with a handful of balloons, asking if someone is calling her. Her name is Hope and she assures the old woman that she is never lost: "Abandoned sometimes, and dashed, but never lost." She asks the old woman what is wrong.

"You see," says the old woman, "I thought I knew who I was and where I was going."

"Who are you?" asks Hope. "And where are you going?"

My director pointed out to me that I was asking the same questions in *Beginnings*. I thought that was interesting – a revelation, in fact.

You have to keep on treating life as an adventure. Someone just pushed you out on a highwire and there's no safety net. Don't look down! Look ahead, and dazzle us all with your footwork. There may be fears that interfere with a successful new career. Fear of rejection. Fear of inability. Fear of competition. Fear of incompetence. Well, I'm not telling you to be unrealistic. No one expects you to *fly* off that highwire. But there's no sense being defeatist either. Don't panic. One step at a time, taken confidently, is going to get you to the other side.

Your maturity is one of your assets. No prospective employer is going to consider you a flighty young thing who's going to drop everything as soon as she finds a man, or worry about you leaving because you're pregnant (heaven forbid!). You can offer your own stability and resolution to succeed as definite pluses. Some of the special emotion reserved for widows also works for you. A widow with a child may be pitied and revered and helped along the way.

Age isn't the problem that it was (though there is still a double standard). However, an older woman may not be able to develop a marketable skill or she may find that she lacks the energy to work full-time. Some of the temporary help firms may be able to place her. Or consider this:

I have mentioned baby-sitters already, and sitting is a friendly, human way to earn extra money. But housekeeping is even more so. Every woman who has run a home of her own has a skill that she can consider selling. Unfortunately in North America today, people tend to look down on housekeepers or maids as "hired help." But they are worth their weight in gold and in very short supply. If you are alone, or have very few ties, you might consider taking on an adopted family. The pay is good, the expenses are nil, and there's built-in company. You'll actually work less than you did as mistress of your own household – there are rules about slave labour which, of course, don't apply to wives. Think about it.

For those women past retirement age who want to keep busy, paid or not, because time hangs heavy on their hands, volunteer jobs have become more and more interesting and challenging. Volunteers are much in demand and are always welcome.

If you lack the energy to do volunteer work on a regular basis, but would still love to do something if only to keep up with other human beings, there are still things you can do.

Perhaps you have a skill that is of use to someone. When I was first married, the dean of women at my college asked me if I would help some newly arrived Chinese students who were having trouble with idiomatic English. My husband was taking a night course, so my students came to me on the night he was out, and we launched their indoctrination. I did it for nothing, that is, no money, but I gained a great deal from it. I made new friends. You could do that. If you were a teacher, or even if you weren't, you could discuss the vagaries of our silly language with some young new Canadians, and you might even offer them some comforting advice about survival while you're at it.

The old golden rule still applies. When you're feeling rotten yourself, try to reach out to help someone else who feels rotten. You'll feel better making them feel better. There are still things you can do for other people which will make you feel valuable and useful. There are a lot of shut-ins now, right across the country, and some of them are on accessible lists. The Meals on Wheels organizations have such lists; nursing homes have waiting lists, government welfare organizations have lists. Ask if you can volunteer to phone a few people, keep in touch with them, check on their health, chat and gossip and spend the time of day with them – by telephone. You can still talk, can't you? It's perfectly possible to make a good friend by voice alone. For that matter, it's possible to turn your friendly tongue into a paying proposition. There used to be a service in Toronto known as Tele-Check, which provided a daily phone call to a shut-in five days or seven days a week. In the case of no answer, the Tele-Check person then made a further appropriate phone call, either to the manager or superintendent of the building in which the shut-in lived, or to a neighbour, friend, or relative. Now this service is duplicated by a 24-hour electronic device called ProtectAlert, with a human being on call (1-800-387-1215). Life consists of more than breathing; and it's nice to spend your breath on conversation once in a while. You might consider some kind of human service in your town or city and earn a little money yourself without leaving home. You charge so much per phone call, or a flat rate per week. It's wise, though, to make the arrangements with a relative of the shut-in. Some people don't appreciate paid friendship and I can't say that I blame them. No one ever said old age was easy.

There are several helpful hints I can pass on to a working widow, which like everything else in these scattered pages I found out the hard way. The first is that you're going to get tired, tired as you have never been. There are times when it will seem that there is no respite. You will have gone the second mile and still there is no haven in sight. Well, weariness is like pain in many respects: you have to give in to it. Ride with it. Don't be ashamed to crawl into bed after dinner. Sometimes an hour is all you need. Sometimes it pays to go to bed early and stay there until morning.

There are so many times when you have to keep on working, running as you do from the job, the paying one, to another, the cooking and bottle-washing one, that it would be wise to recognize the times when you can afford to goof off. Who says the sheets have to be changed every Saturday, or whenever you used to change them? All the rules laid down in housekeeping books and the women's magazines were written for someone else, someone with more time, more leisure, more devotion to good housekeeping than you now have – and more money. So what if the place doesn't get dusted as often? No one pays anything, even attention, to a dusty coffee table. If you're a compulsive housekeeper, then of course you're going to ignore my advice, but if you are feeling guilty because you're not doing what you think someone else thinks you should be doing, then forget it.

I'm not recommending that you turn into a slob. What I am trying to do is absolve you from compulsive housekeeping. I used to be a compulsive housekeeper. I like to call myself a comfortable one now. My aim is to create a comfortable home not a showcase.

One of the sad, ironic advantages of having no husband is that there is no one you think you are failing when you are less than perfect. You're not disappointing anyone if the place isn't spotless by 5 P.M. each day. It's unlikely that your children will even notice. I do have one terribly tidy child, grown now, who, when she comes home to visit, tidies everything in sight until it's out of sight. I can't find anything for days after she's gone. If you have one of these and it's live-in, bear with it and be grateful.

Guilt, it seems, is an occupational hazard of being a woman. One of the things that is going to happen to you, as you rush about doing what is uppermost and demands to be done, is that you will feel guilty about the less demanding things, including children, that just wait there to be attended to. I'm a prime sufferer myself. I always used to feel guilty if my kids were working and I wasn't, though I found they didn't seem to feel at all guilty when I was up and about and they were stretched out in front of the television set.

If you feel guilty about how different, how much more comfortable and secure your children's lives might have been if you weren't working and neglecting them, stop it. The if-onlies can take you right back to Self-Pity, maudlin variety. Life isn't the same, it never will be, and all the if-onlies in the world won't change it. Be grateful you have your children and think of what character they're building. You're building a little character yourself, and you're going to need it because women live a long time. Alone.

A little healthy neglect really doesn't hurt a child, not if he learns independence. Bake a pan of brownies once in a while as an unlooked-for bonus. Chocolate addicts never feel neglected when they're eating brownies.

On the other hand, you mustn't feel like a martyr. It's not only bad for your character, it's also very hard to live with. Give your kids a break as well as yourself. Have a little fun once in a while. It'll do you all good.

Your ego is something that you as a widow have to be careful of. It tends to wither, like a flower without sunshine. You have no one to tell you when you're doing a good job or, for that matter, when you're being a darn fool. Lack of feedback can be very damaging to the psyche. You lose your self-image. That's why, whether it's necessary or not, it's actually valuable to a newly single person to go to work. Work guarantees contact with other people. Work can be the biggest morale-lifter you can find. Work provides focus, a chance to get out of the silent house, to become a functioning independent human being in your own right. "Work keeps at bay three great evils," wrote Voltaire, "boredom, vice, and need." A widow would do well to keep all three at bay.

Once in a while, unbidden, a feeling of accomplishment will arise, and this enables you to square your shoulders and keep on keeping on. There's nothing wrong with a little healthy self-congratulation every now and then. It's a whole lot better than guilt. No one ever said you had to be superlady, but once in a while you feel like it. Go ahead. You're entitled.

# 7

# Children

*Ring around a rosie,*
*A pocket full of posies,*
*Husha, husha.*
*We all fall down.*

*Nursery rhyme*

Even in this day and age, protected as we are from death, children know about it, sing about it, play games with it, honour it. This nursery rhyme comes from the time of the Great Plague when sniffing a posy was believed to offer protection against the unseen killer which decimated the population of London in the seventeenth century. "We all fall down," of course, means we all die. And we all do, sooner or later.

I believe that adults have no right to hide death from children. It is a terrible thing to lie to them.

I was seven when my grandfather died and I knew nothing about it. One day I was taken to see grandma's new home, a comfortable apartment, but there was no room for grandpa and no sign of him either.

"What about grandpa?" I remember asking. "Where will he sleep?" And I was told that grandpa had gone away on a long trip and wouldn't be back. What a rotten thing to do, running out on grandma like that! And it was so unlike him. That wasn't fair, not to tell me. I don't remember how old I was before I finally realized grandpa was dead. By the time I knew, he was a fading memory and I was robbed of awe and grief at his death.

Surely with the death of someone as close as a father, there can be no avoidance of the fact. But how well it is handled depends on the age of the child and on the emotional health of the mother. One week after Bill's death, on the Sunday, I drove the children out to the cemetery after church just so we could check in private on what we had left in a crowd at the funeral. The flowers were dead and there was no tombstone.

"Well, there it is," I said. "You see, he's not here. His body is here and we pay it respect."

I do believe that, but I am reminded of a passage in Pearl Buck's book *A Bridge For Passing*, about the death of her husband, in which she recalled her mother's grief at the death of Pearl's brother. A friend said something about the body being merely the earthly remains, that the child's spirit was safe in heaven. And Pearl's mother replied that the body was all she had left, the body she had borne and nursed and cared for. She has a point. Bill is not in the cemetery; he's closer to me at home, or anywhere I go. But oh, how I miss that body!

Anyway, we didn't have the body to gaze at. We had a muddy pile of earth. Everyone nodded silently at what I had said, and they all looked suitably respectful. We were dry-eyed. Kate broke the silence with a question:

"What's his address?"

We all laughed. Bless her!

"Range 16, lot 43," I said, and we were released.

Laughter can be just as valid a cry of anguish as tears. It's easier (sometimes) to laugh than it is to cry, and it's much more socially acceptable. I know that, but where did my children learn it so young? Laughter is a mask for pain. Sometimes laughter enables you to get closer to the hurtful point than tears ever will. Tears soften and blunt the edges of pain; that's why they are so useful and must be welcomed when they come.

Crying helps. Help your children to cry. Girls and boys. Maybe especially boys, because there still is this stigma attached to masculine tears that they must be helped over. Tears are still the safest release. I'm not saying you have to drown in them, but a few moist eyes early on can brighten the vision later. Help your children to deal with strong feelings. Help them to cry. But laughter makes reality bearable – in short doses – until reality can be faced altogether.

Between the ages of three and five there is an inability to understand death, to conceive of it as a permanent thing. You will be required to give the facts, and to keep on giving them, for as long as the child must hear them. It is a crucial age at which to lose a parent. In a study by psychiatrist Dr. Michael Rutter, reported in Sula Wolff's book *Children Under Stress*, it was found that "the loss of a parent at three or four years is especially damaging because this is the time at which parents are most needed as models for identification."

Somewhere you will have to find a role model for your young sons, perhaps your own brother, if you have one, or brother-in-law, or a cousin, or your father, or a friend of your husband's. At whatever age, sons are terribly vulnerable to their widowed mothers. You must start early to distance yours enough to stand free of you.

Sula Wolff also writes, however, "that the death of a mother generally leads to a greater disruption of the family than the death of a father." If you've been getting the subliminal message from some people that the wrong person died (yes, that too!) tell them that.

Between the ages of five and nine, children develop a gradual acceptance of death as a permanent thing that happens to everyone. They will still want to talk about it a lot. Don't change the subject. Explain the facts. Be open and honest about the cause of death. They will be less frightened than if you shroud it in secrecy.

At this age a child might harbour some feelings of guilt if he or she was ever angry at the deceased. Children have a very direct apprehension of cause and effect and have been known to blame themselves for a death in the family, especially a sudden death, and especially if, in the few weeks before the death, they happened to have shouted in anger: "I hate you. I wish you were dead." Guilt and fear may get all mixed up in their heads, and you'll have to help them over it. It's important to talk about it.

Then, too, children may feel anger at being left. Why not? Lots of mothers feel angry at being left. It helps to talk about it. He didn't mean to go away and leave you. He couldn't help it. Don't blame him.

And if by chance he did mean it, if he committed suicide, then you still mustn't be angry. Help the children to feel sympathy for the pain and despair and anguish that forced him to such an act. Don't blame him.

But don't blame God either. If you have a faith, find a way to explain death (and life) without implicating God as the villain. If you have honest doubts, express them. Don't be afraid to say, "I don't know." How fortunate you are if you have a strong faith and can communicate your belief to your children!

"God needed him." Have you heard that line? Or – and this is worse – "God punished him." You might not say that one, but pray that your children don't overhear someone else saying it. Death is not a punishment for sin. *Everyone dies*. Make sure your children understand that.

By the time they're older, children may not turn so freely to their mother to discuss their father's death. It's important that you keep on talking about him – easily and naturally and lovingly. No one else will. People don't seem to want to talk about someone after he dies. It's as if the earth had swallowed him up and he never existed at all. Well, if he didn't exist, where did all these children come from? Stay open. Be accessible. Make sure your children understand that they can talk if they want to talk. Talk a lot. Keep on talking, whatever age they're at. And remember this: Children need large doses of tender loving care.

So do mothers.

Now, having gotten all soft and mushy, let me warn you not to be too soft. Don't cling. Don't smother. Especially your sons. Sula Wolff warns of this: "Clinging mothers, especially to sons, impede the child's growing up process. Some sons can be handicapped by it, too concerned for the widowed mother." Sometimes you have to discourage their concern for you.

One Saturday night that first summer, it happened that both the girls were out, Matt was invited to a friend's for the night, and John was going to a movie. He was the last one out of the house and hesitated as he said goodbye, realizing in the same instant that I would be alone for the evening.

"Would you rather I stayed home?" he asked.

"That's the last thing I want," I said. "Get out of here." You have to do that. In a way, in time, you have to become less of a mother.

It's called being androgynous and it goes hand in hand with becoming the breadwinner, the head of the house, the decision-maker. As you develop your so-called "masculine" qualities of energy, independence, aggressiveness, you will tend to repress the feminine. That's what I mean when I say you become less of a mother. You have to become both mother and father to your children. Again, it isn't easy.

If, however, you have troubles with your children that you feel you cannot handle, there are experts who can help you when the printed word fails and you desperately need to talk to someone. Start with the teacher, if your child is of school age. The teacher knows the kid better than anyone and may be able to help you with your problem. Try your minister, or Sunday School teacher, if you are a regular church attender, or the Scoutmaster or Brown Owl, if your child attends such a group.

You will discover how very kind other people can be. Different friends took my younger son to the Father and Son Banquet at Scouts each year. Both boys' camp directors were wonderfully kind and helpful. Matt's Big Brother was a joy and a wonder. In fact, the Big Brothers movement is a joy and a wonder, reaching out as it does to help fatherless boys between the ages of six and sixteen. There are times when, as a single parent, you find it impossible to be in two places at once. That's when friends from many sources step into the breach and help. If never before, you learn to receive gratefully and to say thank you from the bottom of your heart.

If you have a son under sixteen years of age do try to get a Big Brother for him. The time he gives to your son is valuable to you in more ways than one. When you are responsible for everything your children do, the relief you feel when someone else takes over, if only for a couple of hours, has to be experienced as it cannot be described. The Big Brother may become the role model your child needs and that's really important. Not to forget that there is the female counterpart in Big Sisters, of which I have no personal experience or knowledge. My daughters had a parent of the same sex – not that I ever claimed to be a role model!

Don't, whatever you do, hold up their missing father as the model your children must live up to. That's blackmail. Don't ever say, "Your father would be disappointed in you." Don't even hint that the child is not living up to his non-existent father's expectations of him. There is no answer a child can give to that and you have saddled him with guilt and posthumous resentment that he can't get rid of. The only way I conjure up their dead father to my children is in a positive way. I say, "Your father would be proud of you," or, "He'd be happy to see you doing so well."

Tempting as it may be, don't tell your son that he's the man of the house now. Other people will anyway, so you don't have to emphasize it. He'll feel his responsibility keenly as it is; try not to rush him out of childhood any faster than he has already been pushed. By the same token, don't expect your young daughter to be "mommy's littler helper." She's still a child and she's the one who needs help, and needs a mother. Don't turn her before her time into a confidante. Friend, yes, but respect her youth and your own maturity. I have seen examples of such mislaid pressure bend some young girls out of their minds, literally.

Your children necessarily will assume more responsibility in their lives than they might have. They will be on their own sooner and they will be doing more for themselves – and for you. I can say don't burden your older children with too much responsibility but it's hard not to. Certainly there is added pressure on them if you have to work to supplement your income. You must rely on your children's co-operation. The danger is that you will lean on them too heavily. Kids are kids and they still have to be respected as such. Sure, they'll pitch in and put dinner in the oven, make a salad, set a table, run errands to the store, clean up after a meal or help with the cleaning and laundry, and God bless them for it. But don't ask them to make the decisions, plan the menus, or remember what to do without written memory jogs. Or hang up their clothes.

What about money? What provision is there for your dependent children in the event of your death before they are ready to leave the nest? Is your income dependent upon your life or is it in trust or investments that are available to your family as well? Certainly your job income will cease if you should die now, and so would your husband's survivor's pension payable to the widow only. If too many sources dry up, then consider term insurance (page 49) on your life to keep your children afloat until they are self-sufficient.

Give a thought to their education. In widows' surveys this was the area that altered most dramatically with the death of the father. The fact is that your children will bear more or most, if not all, of the cost of their education themselves. Most provinces still have a system of (shrinking) loans and grants. They're harder to come by, but ask at your universities and colleges about the bursaries, loans, grants, scholarships – whatever is available – and ask for application forms. This time, your kids will be doing the asking; it's their future they're asking about. Psychologists have proved that anxiety and tension improve learning ability – another ironic advantage of bereavement.

We have already recognized the fact that bereavement is usually accompanied by a substantial drop in income. This can affect children in more ways than the obvious one. They are deprived not only of some of the material benefits they had when their father was alive but also a great deal of their mother's time. Because in her attempts to fill in the money gap she runs out of time for them. There is less money for toys and treats and trips but there is also less time for inexpensive pleasure outings and for bedtime stories, homework help, and games. In other words, no one is having any fun, least of all you.

That's one of the sadder continuing facts of widowhood. You're not having any fun any more. The person who made life most interesting for you and with whom you most liked to have fun is gone. No one else is going to go out of his way to see that you have any fun. So you're going to have to manufacture your own.

Your children are going to feel the same way. Not only is half the source of their comfort, well-being, and fun gone, but the one who's left is a lot more sour and serious than they ever remember her being. Small wonder. You were never scared and lonely before. Well, share your loneliness with the kids. Take time to go on a picnic with them, or to a movie, or to have Chinese food sent in, whatever. Do a jigsaw puzzle, go for a bike ride or cross-country skiing, make popcorn, watch a video together, explore a new park. Your solutions need not be expensive. They just have to be done together. You'll find that your children are delightful people to be with, and it's so very comforting to be with people who really love you – very good for the soul and the ego.

Do something else for your children. Have a party. It's good therapy for you and it's good psychology for them. Show them that good times can still happen, even though their father is gone. Have a family sleighride, or take a bunch of kids tobogganing or skating and bring them back for hot apple cider and hamburgers or lasagna or something. Or have a backyard barbecue in the summer.

Show your children that you care. Listen to them. Do not judge – "That's a terrible thing to say!" Do not stifle them – "You mustn't think things like that!" Help them to articulate their feelings. Recognize anger if it exists and help them to talk it out. Fear too.

It was several months before Kate and I confessed to each other that every time we burped we waited for eight minutes to see if we would die. Sudden death can leave residual fear like that. Death can happen so easily. You have to learn to trust life again, and help your children to trust, too. Death is not necessarily catching.

Perhaps all of us felt the apprehension that Matthew voiced. He was nervous about leaving me to go back to school the day after the funeral. He was afraid, I guess, that I might drop dead, too, and what was there in his experience to say this might not happen? We all took an extra day off together before we parted to resume our lives again.

Matt was in a Special Education class. I phoned his teacher and warned her of his fear. She discussed his situation with the other children in the class and tried to prepare them for a normal reception of him. It was too much to expect. Not knowing what to say, they said nothing, and avoided him. He came home feeling like a social outcast. Grownups also do that, too, say nothing, because they don't know what to say. It's better to speak. Words don't lie as heavy in the air as silence does.

There was only one child who broke the boundaries of fair play with Matt, and I guess he had problems of his own.

"Yah, yah," he shouted at Matt one day. "I'm better than you. I have a father and you don't. Yah, yah." That's unanswerable. (But I have the feeling that some women think that about me and my lack of a husband.)

Children, in short, will go through the same stages of shock, rage, fear, and withdrawal that their bereaved mother does. If you can help them through it, you will perhaps not only shorten their mourning period, you may also help yourself. As a widow, of course, you are harder hit than your children. You have lost the companion of your life, your mate, your lover, your best friend (haven't you?). Your grief will affect the whole household, and will continue to do so when you have attacks of it.

Oddly enough, however, or perhaps not oddly at all, just as a widow who has survived an unhappy marriage will be more badly affected by the death of her husband, so will her children be less able to handle the bereavement. Again, it is the grief and guilt of the mother that affect the children. If you have such a problem you'll have to work out your hostility for the sake of your own mental health, but I pray that you do not turn your hostility on the children. They need you, as whole and loving as you can be.

You must learn to share with your children – your sorrow, satisfactions, some of your worries, your self – without leaning on them too heavily. Their lives have changed, too; you can't protect them from the world any more. The world has already happened to them. Go ahead and communicate with them, and expect a lot. They can deliver more help, common sense, and practical solutions than you could have imagined. Just don't frighten them. You're the adult; keep it that way. You make the decisions, inform them of your plans but don't expect them to plan for you. You can't opt out that easily. You're the head of the household now. Act like it.

Now if I sound awesomely tough and mature, let me quickly confess that there have been many times when I have broken down and been the recipient of comfort from my children. My youngest used to leave his place at the table and come to pat my arm if he saw weather warnings in me. In the first weeks and months when I continued to try to take the walks Bill and I were accustomed to taking on Sunday afternoons, Matt would leave his friends and run after me to tag along. And the older children would spot my lonely times and one or the other of them would wander into the living room and offer to talk. I learned more about electronics and stereo equipment and physics from John than I ever expected to know. But they also helped more with chores than they ever did and provided companionship as well as assistance. There was a kind of bittersweet compensation in this. They didn't have to share me with my husband any more. Perhaps that is a saving grace, that although they no longer had two parents, they had access to the undivided attention of one – when they could catch me.

One other thing I have to bring up: dating. That is an old-fashioned word, and there is much more said about it in another chapter, but you should give a thought to how it affects the children because it will in turn affect you. Little children often feel threatened by their mother's dating. They are afraid she will be taken away from them, or else they resent a father figure, if the man in question attempts to come on too strong as an authority. Teenaged children feel threatened too, particularly a boy who regards himself in some way as the man of the house.

As for Mother, she feels like an overgrown teenager herself. Very odd. I mean, theoretically, you can stay out as late as you want because you're grownup and you don't have a curfew, but can you really face your kids if you stay out till four in the morning? I couldn't. I'm still Mother.

Older children feel somewhat proprietary about their widowed mothers. A few I have spoken to are genuinely happy for their parent when she finds another interest, whether it's a round-the-world cruise, a good job, or a new husband. But many adult children are fearful that a new man in their mother's life is merely after her money – I mean, he couldn't possibly be interested in her in a man-woman relationship, could he? (He could.) The commonest reaction to a new man is a well-hidden, latent jealousy. An older widow's decision to remarry can bring back painful memories of the bereavement that left her thus available. As long as she was faithful to her husband's memory, father was still around, in a way. Even at this late stage in life, a son or daughter may feel rejected by the mother's insistence on having a life of her own. If any of these reactions occur in your life, you will find they're harder to deal with than with the bewildered grief of a five-year-old. But you will have to deal with the problem. All I can say is, keep the lines of communication open.

Something I didn't know to tell when I first wrote this book (so many things I didn't know!) was what happens to daughters who have lost their fathers at an early age. A young girl misses out on that first male to cut her teeth on, to relate to as a buddy, and to respond to as an admirer. If she has no brother(s), she may not learn any male-female camaraderie at all, and she has no evidence of the easy, friendly, give-and-take of a companionable, long-term relationship that two intact parents might have given her. But that's nothing compared to the anxiety I witnessed in my daughters when they first fell in love. They were terrified of what would happen to them when that love ended – through death. They couldn't bear the thought of experiencing what they had seen at first-hand in their mother. Both of them reported a dark night of the soul while they struggled with a more poignant, frightening side of love than most young women are even aware of. Try to be prepared for that, as I was not, and be ready to assure them that it was worth it. It was, wasn't it?

Your relationship with your grown children is at once a personal and a contemporary problem. The extended family of past generations is no longer popular. The myth is that widowed grandmothers and maiden aunts and dotty uncles and spinster sisters used to live together and share the child care and chores with the mother and father in houses big enough to accommodate all of them. Daughters and sons today are not too eager to have a widowed mother live with them in smaller quarters, and she is often fiercely independent and wants to do for herself in her own place as long as she can. By 1991, 1.3 million Canadian women lived alone, 38 per cent of them sixty-five and over, as opposed to only 15 per cent of the men this age. (Interestingly, the percentage of divorcées versus widows has almost exactly reversed since the thirties, with divorced women now in the majority.) Most older single women prefer to live alone until they can no longer take care of themselves. Apparently, the level of income dictates the solitary lifestyle rather than the number of children one has. Your arrangements will depend on your financial situation, your health, and your relationship with your children.

"It's harder for older widows," an older widowed aunt wrote to me, "than for young ones, for you are still needed. That is the most difficult adjustment to make – to have no one to whom you are absolutely essential." She was right. I was lucky that I was not left alone, although my anxiety for my children's future often made their dear presences a mixed blessing. I often realized, however, that I needed my children more than they needed me, more so as they have grown up and cleaved, as they say, to families of their own. I took care, and I continue to take care, not to let my need overwhelm them.

One by one my children left home. Only when the last one left did I feel a loss of my own identity, and some guilt, but that was a special case. I had had to work very hard to make it possible for him to leave and be independent (see *The Book of Matthew*). I was not as disturbed by the departure of the fledglings from the nest as other women I knew. One mother said to me when our first daughters went off to college: "Isn't it terrible, that empty place at the dinner table?" I didn't remind her I already had an empty place.

I was not as disturbed because I had this larger departure I was and still am coping with. At least my children are still on this earth. I can phone them and they can visit and I can talk to them. And hug them. That helps.

What you do for your children is what you must do for yourself. Face the facts. Reality hurts, but hiding from it is going to hurt more in the long run. Share your sorrow. Support each other in your grief. Your children, no matter what their ages, are the only people in the world who come close to knowing how bad it is, who have a loss almost as deep as yours. Care for them and share yourself. If you can, share faith and hope as well. Assert your faith by making an effort. Try to make things better for your children because of the insight you've gained. Love them and thereby honour the person whose loss you share.

# 8

# Companionship

*So far as is known,
no widow ever eloped.*

E.W. Howe

Walk through any cemetery with tombstones in it dating from before the turn of the century and you will see the social change which has led to the situation of widows in North America today. In the dim dark days before antisepsis, women often died in childbirth, so it was not uncommon for a man to outlive two or three wives. A man can still have two or three wives, but it's called divorce and it's much more messy and expensive. Now women are outliving men because someone thought of washing his hands before delivering a baby.

And then there's the apparent death wish of the North American male, expressed in killing expense accounts, high living, dumb eating habits, not enough exercise, too many business pressures. If the feminist movement manages to relieve men of some of the pressures and responsibilities of making it in the world today, and thereby enables them to live a little longer and keep women company a little longer, that would be a great achievement. Because women today face, increasingly, a great portion of their lives without men.

The average age at which a woman is widowed is still fifty-six; the average life expectancy of a girl child born today is eighty-one years. A woman who is sixty-five today can expect to live another nineteen years, and an eighty-six-year-old woman has a fifty-fifty chance of another six and a half years! Although more Canadian women are marrying for a second or third time, nine out of ten times they are divorcées, not widows. Fewer than one in ten widows marry again, not only because no one asked them. Any way you look at it, women have a long time to go on alone.

Well-meaning friends have probably told you that you'll get married again, as if that were the solution to all your problems. You know better. As with your insurance policies, you have to consider your options. Marriage is merely one of them, perhaps the least likely, though this may take a while to sink in.

But you should think about it. Work your way through it and come to a decision so that you are whole and secure within yourself. Think about whether you want to risk your emotions and your life on another marital venture. One widow said to me: "I have not yet met a man with whom I want to spend more than three or four hours – the length of time it takes to eat a good dinner."

There are several stereotypes about widows: there is the biblical widow, poor and sorrowing, with her widow's mite and her struggle to survive. There is the sex-mad, wealthy widow of a simpler society (Shakespeare's plays are full of eager widows), when widows were not such a bad catch. If a widow had children, she had proved her fertility and ability to survive childbirth when it was still economically advantageous to have children. She usually had some property or money, never a bad thing, and her sexual expertise had to be assumed. Today, sexual expertise is rampant, widows are a glut on the market, and wealthy ones are rare.

By Victorian times, following the lead of the widowed queen who went into a state of paralysis after Albert died, widows were swathed in black and left high, dry, respectable, and neglected in cold parlours with their sewing, their grandchildren, and other widows – they have so much in common! They were supposed to live on their memories and be grateful.

A combination of these attitudes still exists about widows. Widows are supposed to be retroactive vestal virgins, keeping alight the memorial candle and protecting the flame of fidelity even after death has parted the twain. It's not fair, of course.

I speak to a lot of widows in the course of my work, and every year I seem to hear more stories that enforce my conviction that it's unfair, that the ghetto we've been thrust into is stifling, that the expectation that we will live out the remainder of our lives in uncomplaining celibacy is harsh and unfeeling. No one puts black wreaths on the door any more; why should we have black veils swathed around our sexuality?

It may be an insoluble problem, however. At least recognize that it *is* a problem. Don't comfort yourself that only 32 per cent of widows are under the age of sixty-five and that the other 68 per cent don't have a problem. That's another stereotype: the blue-haired sixty-five-year-old widow with her rings and her poodle, content to eat and gossip and live out her life on the vicarious kicks and lollipop thrills of Harlequin romances. At least they offer safe sex!

The double standard of aging is very hard on widows. Shere Hite, in her best-selling study of women's sexuality, *The Hite Report*, says: "For centuries it has been a hideous cliché in our culture that older women are not sexual women." Society would prefer to believe that older woman are asexual. Women know better. Even when they are well past the menopause, women still see themselves as sensual, sexual human beings. According to the women surveyed in *The Hite Report*, the enjoyment of sex heightens and the capacity for it increases with age. Women in their late sixties and early seventies reported both interest and aptitude. As the greeting card puts it more truly than Hallmark realizes: "You're not getting old, dearie, you're getting better!" But what good does it do you if you're alone?

While mature men are not blamed for taking young wives, an older woman – that is, any woman over forty – is supposed to be grateful if a spry seventy-year-old gives her the nod. I actually received a proposal of marriage on a open-line radio show from a seventy-one-year-old caller who needed someone to cook and clean for him. "What are you offering in return?" I asked.

As Susan Sontag put it in her devastating essay *The Double Standard of Aging*, "A woman knows that should she re-enter the sexual market at a later date – because of divorce, or the death of her husband, or the need for erotic adventure – she must do so under a handicap far greater than any man of her age (*whatever* her age may be) and regardless of how good-looking she is."

Not that widows don't get sexual offers. They do, but they're generally from married men. A whole survey could be devoted to the lines men use with widows. It's a different approach. The general theme is selflessness. Any widow will tell you (they've told *me*) that the male attitude toward a widow is purely altruistic, although men do tend to expect more than their due of gratitude for whatever services they offer. Most men, in fact, are surprised when most widows say no. *No thank you*. Men like to think of themselves as social workers performing a needed service. Sexual social workers.

One gets offers from the most bizarre sources, leading one to suspect that the motivation is not really pity but the prospect of a new kick. Not that it's easy to storm the bastions. Widows are highly vulnerable and they can sometimes be taken once or even twice because of that vulnerability, but they get gun-shy pretty fast.

The first time I had hands laid on me in lust and not in love, I cried a lot. Forgotten tremors can trigger responses that are difficult to control. They have, however, a therapeutic effect. They complete the sexual mourning process.

"There is no sanctuary," wrote Cyril Connolly, "in one bed from the memory of another." One widow reported to me that she couldn't reach a climax with her first lover A.D. She enjoyed the loving and the cuddling, but she just couldn't let go. Does anyone remember the film *A Man and a Woman*? A divorced man and a widow who think they have fallen in love try to go to bed, but she finds she can't make it. The memory of her husband – more than memory – his imprint – is all over her body. She cries, and the man withdraws, helpless and defeated by a ghost. When one has been married for a long time, one retains a married psyche for a long time. It takes a while to become a single woman again, no longer a wife.

Perhaps that is one reason why widows, even though they are lonely, hold out. Sociologist Paul Bohannan estimates that one-fifth of widows and one-tenth of divorcées experience more than three years' abstinence before resuming sexual relationships. Widows, particularly, feel they are being faithful still – even to a memory – and find it difficult to take that first giant step into an alien bed.

I know it's fear. My own wound remained so raw for

so long, I couldn't let go. Even when I thought I had found someone, I was reticent, playing push-me-pull-you games. I am still terrified of what another loss could do to me. I think I can stand anything, but why put myself out for such pain? I found that my feeling has been duly recognized by psychiatrists. It is called a "phobic response to marriage" and is experienced by women who lost their mates without warning. It affects the nature of eventual recovery. Yes indeed.

But you still need companionship. Fortunate are you if you can find someone who will be satisfied with the lemonade kisses and milk-and-water hugs of your youth (if your youth was in fact milk-and-water), that is, a platonic companion. And fortunate, too, if that's all *you* want. Try as one will to live a spiritual life, one still has a physical body that is comforted by human contact. It's another of the inexorable problems of widowhood that must be dealt with. Obviously, you're not going to be able to live with yourself in a state of promiscuity (are you?), but you have this devastating hunger.

If and when a widow starts seeing other men, she must overcome a feeling of disloyalty. She has no one left to be faithful to, and that is a disconcerting realization. It's as if she has lost her anchor, her touchstone, her safety zone – all of that. "I want someone to hold me," one young widow wrote to me, and her feeling is shared by most widows. It isn't always a sexual feeling. It's the human need, not limited to children, to be cradled, to be comforted, to be hugged. I'm not the only one who goes around saying how necessary hugs are for human beings. But sex is important, too.

"Widows are so gullible," an older widow wrote me, "that anything in pants looks good after a while!"

One's needs, after all, must be reconciled with one's morality. It depends on one's personal attitudes (and religion) as to which is easier to bear – guilt or frustration. Often religion serves only to complicate matters, not to resolve them. One widow came up to me after a seminar I was conducting on companionship and second marriages.

"My doctor says I should have an affair," she said, "that it would do me a world of good. I told my minister that and he said, 'You know what our religion thinks of that.' What should I do?" She was asking me a direct question I hadn't yet learned how to handle for myself. I told her what the semanticist Korzybski said: "God may forgive you, but your nervous system won't." That didn't help much, I guess, but it's true. In the end, you have to do what you are comfortable with. You have to give yourself permission to behave according to what makes you most comfortable, whether it's celibacy or not. You're the one you have to live with.

Some widows, of course, hope to remarry. I used to think I would. I was good at marriage, I thought, having had a successful one. But many of the men I met weren't good at it, being battle-scarred and scared survivors of messy, bitter divorces and queasy, addictive separations. Trust doesn't come so easily then, and pain does. The few widowers I met were victims of great expectations or of bad timing.

Timing truly is everything, for all concerned. It is quite true that most widows get more offers (but not of marriage) than they ever accept. That's almost another cliché. But the offers they accept get little acknowledgment. Most of them are horror stories.

The horror lies in the fact that the two principals want different things. The widow, like most women, wants tender loving care, some undivided attention, concern, and affection, not necessarily marriage (believe it or not). The man wants . . . something else. He claims to be helping her, but it is really himself he is servicing.

The one fact that emerges again and again from all

the stories I hear is that a widow can't be too careful. It wouldn't be a bad idea for a widow to run a credit rating on every man she goes out with, and I'm talking about character credit, not money – though it wouldn't be so dumb to check out his finances as well. I have learned of widows who signed over their businesses, their houses, their housekeeping services, and their bodies to fast, sweet-talking men who were going to "look after them." I know one widow, a younger woman, who had actually moved in with a man and his three children. He was in the process of getting a divorce, he told her, so he could marry her. She was housekeeper and babysitter and mistress. He asked her to move out but to come in by the day for the child-care so he could list her as a house-keeper and not jeopardize the divorce proceedings. Well, he got his divorce and promptly got married – to someone else.

Another widow wrote me that she had had four affairs since her husband's death three years earlier, including a fairly lengthy one with a divorced man who moved into her house with his children. Hers and his fought.

There's another consideration. Even if a widow is prepared to take a chance herself, she must think about her children, especially if they are still at home. Person-ally, I never liked the thought of waking up in the morn-ing and introducing my children to the man in bed beside me, nor would I have been any happier as the strange lady in some daddy's bed, ready for a spurious togetherness at a family breakfast. That takes more poise than I like to think most people can muster.

Another widow I know met a charming divorced man (there may be a shortage of widowers, but there's no shortage of divorced men these days). She noticed that when he played with his children, invariably one or the other of them got hurt, painfully, to the point of tears. It was always "accidental" but it happened with surprising frequency. The man just didn't seem to know his own strength or how to curtail it in horseplay with his little ones. Then, by chance, my acquaintance met a woman who was a friend of the man's ex-wife, so close a friend, in fact, as to have been the one who took her in when her husband beat her up. A widow – or any woman, for that matter – has the right to expect that a man she goes out with (or marries) hasn't hit a woman since he was in sixth grade.

I know widows who have met men at singles' bars and I know a couple of divorcées who have advertised (successfully) in the personal column for a companion. There is one little catch to men you meet without any background information from friends or business associates: they're often married. Not unhappily married, either. Happily married and happily looking around.

The moral to all my stories is that it pays to ask questions. Find out. Do a little sleuthing. Make sure you know something about the man before you get hurt or taken or both. Don't go out with a perfect stranger. Remember, no one is perfect. These truths may seem self-evident, but not to a woman long sheltered and newly thrust into a world of singles. Do I have to say more? Yes. You'd think singles bars would be less popular than they used to be, before STDs (Sexually Transmitted Diseases), but they're still one of the most popular meet markets available. There's no such thing as a one-night stand any more, though. As the AIDS warnings point out, if you sleep with someone you don't know very well, you are also going to bed with the last eight or ten people he knew, over the last five to eight years (whichever comes first). That's enough to cool anyone's hot blood.

You may, as I have, met a number of men at friends' houses. Even with a proper introduction in a safe and respectable setting, you still have to be careful. Your friends don't have to be as discriminating as you are. "Dining," as Edna Ferber once observed, "is not mating."

Not that a widow is mating. Far from it. Most of the time she's scared, tired, and reticent. She is not all that eager to raise someone else's children or, if she has come through a terminal illness with her spouse, to nurse another man to his grave. If she has money (some widows do), she is even more at risk. ("She's either a Nurse or a Purse," one bitter woman said to me.) All thoughts of marriage aside, even conversation is difficult. Ten, fifteen, twenty years of marriage spoil one for casual conversations. With a new man there are no comfortable assumptions, no backlog of shared experiences, no tolerance of each other's foibles. "It's easy to make new friends," a friend once said to me, "but hard to make old ones." It's even harder to make old husbands; you have to start several years ago. You did, in fact.

Conversation. Pillow talk. It isn't merely sex that is missing from the lives of women alone. It's friendship, affection, spiritual intimacy – all much more difficult to replace than mere physical contact. Widows who have nursed their husbands through a long illness and who were denied any physical release because of the illness – anywhere from three months to six years – tell me they didn't feel the sexual hunger during that period that they did after their husbands were gone. They still had a companion and some physical contact: the comfort of a kiss, a hug, or a pat, or a hand held in silent understanding.

Many of the women quoted in *The Hite Report* echo this need for touching, for friendly physical contact, for a little loving, a little warmth to make one feel less alone. We're all alone, of course, but widows are more alone, or feel more alone.

111

But there's a reticence about physical contact in our society. Says Shere Hite, "Aside from touching one's partner during sex, it only seems possible to touch children and animals." Are we back to the stereotype of the blue-rinse widow lavishing her affection on her poodle or her cats, or the loving grandmother eagerly baby-sitting all her grandchildren in return for hugs and kisses? Both are acceptable ways of expressing a need and at least partially fulfilling it. What about widows who are younger than that?

I found it very hard to be a widow in one's forties; I used to pray for the sap to stop running. I had a great sex drive and there were times when it drove me up the wall. I think sex is one of the nicest adult games there is, between very close, loving friends, preferably husband and wife. I have come so far in my thinking as to recognize other relationships, and needs. The pleasure of another's mouth and hands and arms is incredibly comforting, also addictive. "We have to think," said Gloria Steinem, "to what extent we have all become man junkies."

I always believed in (a) chastity and (b) fidelity. I married young and fidelity was easy. Chastity is not. I know celibacy never hurt anyone, although the French writer Remy de Gourmont once called it "the last perversion." Nevertheless, like a lot of widows, I never accepted my imposed celibacy easily. But I am of a generation of women who were taught, and most of whom still believe, that the sex act without love is worse than nothing. The physical movements are the external gestures of an emotional and spiritual state called love. With love the gestures are meaningful; without love they are degrading but also, for some and for a time, necessary and helpful – for the short term.

"I went away for a weekend with a man," one not-so-merry widow told me, "thinking I was very free and grown-up. But Monday morning was worse than ever and I hated myself as well."

Another told me she had tried sex-as-release twice and found it hopelessly dissatisfying. "When it's over you miss love," she said. Still another received an unwanted gift from a thoughtless lover – herpes. "I'm lucky it wasn't AIDS," she commented philosophically.

Suddenly celibacy has become more attractive.

Here's a funny point: you call that control and care "chastity" and "fidelity" if you're moral; "celibacy" and "monogamy" if you're hygienic. Same thing.

So I maintain as I did in the dear sheltered days of my one-man marriage that sex without commitment is futile. Harder for me to say now, with my nose pressed against the glass of the candy store, wanting what I haven't got.

There are lots of understanding counsels (including mine) at your nearest library these days, as well as more colourful advice in the women's magazines. What you have to do is re-analyze the role that sex plays or played in your life. Everything else has changed, so maybe this has, too. The nineties are vastly different than any of the last four decades, whenever you formed your opinions and behaviour patterns. You may just be changing your image of yourself, and that is going to affect your relationships with other people, including men.

Generally, widows are not certain of the kind of relationship they want. It's still easiest, perhaps, to say they miss sex and to search for that, and a lot of widows do. Sex is still often the name of the game, the game you have to play to get those other things a widow often wants more: comfort, companionship, cuddling – in short, love. Love is much harder to find than sex. Ingrid

Bengis, author of *Combat in the Erogenous Zone*, writes, "When I love no one it is the absence of love that is more painful than the absence of sex."

I suppose it depends on who you are and where you've been and certainly on how old you are. Widows who have had a good marriage know how important love is, but widows who have had a good marriage also know how important sex is. And we haven't mentioned sin, have we?

Sin is an old-fashioned word these days. It happens that I am religious, with a sense of sin. I understand the meaning of alienation of self from God, and I'd like to avoid that abyss if I can, but it's never been easy. Perhaps you will be comforted, as I have been, by what St. Augustine said so long ago: "Lord grant me chastity and continence, but do not grant them yet." I could always get married again (not likely). But St. Augustine also said, "Second marriages are lawful, but holy widowhood is better." Catch 22.

And what about this terrible, relentless hunger that will not go away? I have talked to widows in their seventies who still feel it. There seems to be no easy solution, not for the million or so women already widowed.

You're going to be all right. Bertrand Russell suggested that women will atrophy and become brittle if they give up sex after having had it for years. David Reuben (of *Everything You Always Wanted to Know About Sex* fame) says much the same thing. Nonsense. There is nothing to get brittle, or rusty, for that matter. If your general health is good, so are your moving parts. You'll be able to deliver if and when you want to.

But your own needs must be recognized. Why do you think those older widows lavish so much love and affection on their dogs and cats? And baby-sit and do volunteer work and teach Sunday school and go to church? All these are acceptable ways of letting off – and receiving – love.

Hugs and kisses are available closer to home when you still have children there. I asked for it, for loving. My older son, at fourteen, was embarrassed the first time I asked him to give me a hug. Matthew, my younger son, never had any problem, because he had never stopped. And my daughters' shoulders seemed at times too young for the burden of grief I was laying on them. But my need for physical reassurance was strong and I got my hugs, and gave them.

I think it's good for the children. Two of mine were possibly not demonstrative by nature, but they learned to handle hugs with a great deal more aplomb. It proved to be a helpful expertise for them to have. And it helped me to sublimate a need.

Sublimate, according to the dictionary, means "to convert the energy of primitive impulses into acceptable social and cultural manifestations." Fortunately, these days, a lot more manifestations are acceptable than they ever used to be! It's still more likely that the limits of your behaviour lie within you and not in the acceptance of society around you.

You still have to convert that energy and find an outlet for those impulses. Exercise helps, in more ways than one. Regular exercise is going to keep you fit and healthy into your old age, and you need every resource, including the physical, that you can lay your hands on. Join a club or a Y, take yoga classes, learn tai chi, good through to old age. Just make sure that you get enough good, hard, regular exercise to convert that energy. If you ever do decide that your primitive impulses deserve some undivided attention, you'll find you have stamina for other things also.

Cherish your friends. I am a closer, better friend to a

lot of people than I ever was in my married life. I need them, and they have made room for me in their lives. But I try to give in return. Marriage, you see, isn't the only close relationship you can have.

Widowhood, it seems, is becoming a complete personality course. (A finishing school?) As you gather all your resources, you become a more complete, self-fulfilling person, never a bad thing. One widow actually said to me, "Isn't it ironic that I had to lose my husband to find myself?" Life is full of such irony.

So you gain strength as you go along, and perspective and new, wider, extended friendships. And the best new friend you have is yourself.

# 9

# Loneliness

*There are days when solitude for someone my age is a heady wine that intoxicates you with freedom, others when it is a bitter tonic, and still others when it is a poison that makes you beat your head against the wall. . . . This evening I would much prefer not to say which it is; all I want is to remain undecided, and not to be able to say whether the shiver that will seize me when I slip between the cold sheets comes from fear or contentment.*

*Colette*

Loneliness is an increasing problem today and is not confined to widows. The high mobility of our society has made deep and lasting friendships difficult to make and maintain. If a couple doesn't have each other, they're in trouble, and frequently they are, as the increasing fragmentation of the family makes clear. There is no doubt, however, that intimate relationships alleviate loneliness. We all know that. We also know that the relationships have to be creative and supportive and based on genuine affection, or they will be damaging. Still, drowning people clutch at straws. It is loneliness that causes a lot of so-called promiscuity among single people (and not only singles!). Sex can provide a short-term spurious intimacy that begins by comforting and ends by alienating people even more. The moral is that we all need love.

This book is really about love. Death wouldn't mean anything if you hadn't loved the one who died. And you are not going to survive now if you do not withdraw that love and aim it elsewhere. Your first target is yourself. If you don't love and accept yourself, you're not going to be able to love others, and you're going to go on being lonely.

First you have to find out who you are. You've been someone else all your life. You were your parents' daughter, your husband's wife, your children's mother. Now you are your own keeper, and a survivor. In spite of all the kindnesses of well-meaning friends and relatives, the one thing they can't do for you is make you grow. In fact, they have a tendency to make you become less than you could be, precisely because they are so kind and well-meaning.

When you lose your husband, you lose your best friend and your sternest critic as well. Lots of people tell you when you look nice, when you've done a good job, when your dessert is delicious, or what a good speech you made. But few people care enough to tell you when you've been a horse's ass. They just let you go on making a fool of yourself. Surely you did that for each other, rode herd, provided a system of checks and balances, offered constructive criticism, blew the whistle when it was time? I hope you did. And that's what you miss when you don't have it any more – feedback. You have to learn to look at yourself.

Know yourself. It's an ancient Greek saw, and it still has a few teeth. Take a good long look at yourself. Pain will have removed a few scales from your eyes, and you should be able to see more clearly. Ask yourself a few questions.

Are you drinking too much? Sorry, but this is a trap a lot of widows fall into: I know several, especially ones who have been well provided for financially. With no pressures driving them out to work, forcing them to focus on something other than themselves, and with no one suffering economically if they spend too much money on booze, they wallow in self-pity and whisky. And most of their friends are too soft-hearted to tell them to snap out of it. Indulgence is not always kind; self-indulgence is downright destructive. Drinking alone and too much is an unproductive activity. You're being a damn fool if that's what you're doing. Stop it.

Quit drinking. Get a job. Go read to a shut-in. Take a trip. Clean your own house. Have a grandchild. Take a Great Books Course. Have an affair!

Which brings us to the next hard question. Are you screwing around? Are you getting known as an easy lay? Are you being, in other words, promiscuous? In Bermuda, there is an expression for this kind of behaviour, which is often characteristic of frantic, frightened widows. It's called "going foolish." Everyone knows you're not in your right mind, but at least try to hang on to your body. Don't go foolish.

Widows are highly vulnerable. I'll be the first to admit that. It's all too easy to drift in and out of one affair after the other, searching for love and picking up a little easy loving. There are a lot of lonely people out there, willing to be partners. And your friends, if they realize what you're doing, will continue to be kind. They'll forgive you, or refuse to judge you in the first place, and point instead to what you've been through,

119

poor dear. You're going to have to be your own judge.

You think you have nothing left to lose, but you have. It's called self-respect. Decide what you want most, then figure out what to do about it.

There are four kinds of relationships, according to psychologists, that mitigate against loneliness. The first is the romantic sexual relationship. If you can rule that one out, at least for the time being, there are still three others that you can work on. These are friendships, family relationships, and personal commitment to a cause, a course of action, a community, a productive type of work, or a social network of some kind. All these are other-directed. Once you have truly learned to love yourself you can turn your capacity for love, tenderness, care, and concern toward others. And you'll make more friends, almost more than you'll have time for; I guarantee it!

There is a difference between loneliness and being alone. Being alone can get to be a habit, a delightful one. Being alone can give you freedom to do what you want; call it self-indulgence if you will. Being alone can encourage self-development and self-reliance as well, both valuable attributes to have. But an attack of loneliness is an assault on your whole system and on the whole careful structure of self-protectiveness you have set up. Though it may occur less and less frequently as time passes, when an attack does come on, like a tidal wave, the shock can carry you gasping and breathless and sobbing right back to the beach where you were first stranded.

First of all, be comforted; it happens to every widow. Next, what are you going to do about it? All your hard won strength has got to be of some use to you now when you need it. In this list-happy, pragmatic world we live in, there are lots of things you can do about it. Consider:

1. Make a list. Write down the times when your lone-

liness strikes and take measures to prevent the next attack. Frequently it's seasonal and you can't do much about it. Anniversaries, birthdays, Christmas, Thanksgiving, private milestones in your life together – these can trigger attacks year after year. Widows who become grandmothers long after their husband's death told me that the birth caused retroactive pain. I had to discover for myself how true that was. I was awake all night while my daughter-in-law was giving birth to her son, my first grandchild. John phoned me in the morning to announce the arrival and to tell me they were naming him William. I knelt to pray my thanks, and wept.

I found weddings more painful than funerals, for very selfish reasons that I'm not proud of. I dampened my best friend's twenty-fifth anniversary when she and her husband renewed their vows in her presence of their families and her only attendant – lugubrious me. Really, you have to watch that you don't wallow. There's not much you can do about something as inexorable as the calendar, except maybe brace yourself and know that this, too, will pass.

But there are other lists you can make, happier ones. Make a list of dinner parties you'd like to have and list the people you'd invite and plan the menus. You may get around to one or none of them but you've had the time-consuming pleasure of planning them. Make a list of all your clothes, from memory, and then make a list of ones you should get rid of and ones you can add something to so that they'll last another season. Make a list of new clothes you'd like to buy. Now make a list of clothes you can afford to buy! You can make Christmas shopping lists in July if you really get going. Once you get the hang of it, you don't need me to help you.

2. Paint a room, or a piece of furniture, or a picture.

3. Clean your oven.

4. Polish the silver.

121

5. With everything so clean, have a party!

6. Cook up a storm – for your party.

7. But if you can't afford to have a party, try cooking something you've never cooked before, something really complicated and creative. Even if you don't feel like eating it when you're done, you had the fun and concentration of doing it.

8. Sew something spectacular. For me it's spectacular if I sew on a button, but I know women who enjoy the challenge of a French couturier design pattern.

9. Do something you've never done before. Make it something you've always had a secret desire to do. Obviously there are financial limitations to this. It isn't likely you can take off on a trip around the world. But maybe you've always been meaning to explore an art gallery and never got around to it. Or take in a local ferry boat ride, or train ride, or some equally obvious local tourist attraction that natives never get around to doing. Do it.

10. Take a trip. Invite yourself somewhere. You must have had friends invite you to come and visit. Take them up on it. You needn't stay long. But a visit with friends will give you a real lift and is guaranteed to dispel loneliness.

11. Write something: a poem? a letter? a diary? That's best of all. As a writer I am addicted to paper, but anyone with a fresh pad of paper and a ballpoint pen can write down what she feels and get it out where she can look at it. That's how Lynn Caine, author of the bestseller *Widow*, which you should read, began to write her book. I find a diary is cheaper than a shrink and it helps to distance the pain a little.

12. Cut your hair, or colour it, or both. Remember that line from Wilde's *The Importance of Being Ernest*? "I hear her hair has turned quite gold from grief." I'm not being as facetious as I sound. Have a facial, a pedicure, a

massage. Pamper yourself, in other words. Do something to make yourself feel good, and to feel good about yourself.

13. Turn your electric blanket on high and go back to bed. Scunge. One widow wrote me that she used to watch the TV Guide and when there was a movie she really wanted to see on the Morning Movie, she would take a breakfast tray back to bed with her and watch it. Why not?

14. Take a course. Join a political party and work for it actively. Read a book. You may pamper your body but you should give your mind a good work-out. Take your mind off your troubles and set it other problems.

15. But give your body a work-out, too. Take up a new sport, or go back to an old one. Take tennis lessons. Start jogging. Swim a mile.

16. Make love. This has its complications and drawbacks, which we have already discussed.

17. Get out of the house. Go to a movie or a singles bar (drink pop if you're nervous). Go on a picnic. Take an historic walk. Go to a concert. Explore something.

18. Crawl into a hole and pull the hole in after you. Sometimes it's so bad that's all you can do. Well, go ahead and brood. Wallow in it. Cry. Feel sorry for yourself. But don't try to share this with anyone. When you're fit for human companionship again, emerge, like a butterfly from a grubby cocoon. Have a hot bath – with bubbles – and you're bound to feel better in half an hour.

19. Scream.

20. Pray.

21. Forgive someone. There's a lot of residual anger flying around in you. When you're in one of these moods pick out someone you really feel resentful of and forgive him or her. Do something for her: bake her a loaf of bread or invite her for lunch or write him a note. Freed

of even a fraction of your burden of anger, you will feel much much better.

22. Make fudge with a child. If you don't have one the right age, borrow one.

23. Get organized. Getting organized takes a lot of time and can usually get you involved enough to tide you over an attack. You can organize your files – you must have files of something you want organized! Sort out your recipes. Save things. Throw things out. Go through all your magazines. Clip things. Write things down. Oh, this will make you feel better!

24. Start a clippings collection: happy or comforting or challenging, poems, quotations, thoughtful letters from people, news items, encouraging words, cartoons, whatever. Paste them in a scrapbook. Then when you're down you can re-read them. That's why people hang posters like one I found which reads:

> I believe in the sun
> Even when it is not shining
> I believe in love
> Even when I am alone
> I believe in God
> Even when He is silent.

25. Go through it. You have to, you know. There's no turning back.

You will have realized, going through this list, that most of the solutions assume a certain amount of energy on your part. What happens if the spirit is young but the flesh is aging and weak? Loneliness is a problem compounded by age. It takes get-up-and-go to make loneliness get up and go. And sometimes it takes money too, more money than you have. There must be ways that an older person can find to ease the bad days without it costing an arm and a leg, or using tired ones. What can you do?

If society tends to ignore widows generally, it especially neglects older ones, trapped by frailty in a lonely room. Unoccupied time hangs heavy, and you are the one who must fill it, moment by moment, day by day.

I knew a woman, a widow, who was trapped by arthritis in a room where she was brought three not-always-inspired meals a day. People who visited her came away with a lift, and so they went back again. She listened to them; she didn't complain about her own aches and pains, which were myriad and severe. She remembered their children's names, and their husbands', and asked after them. She was glad to see them when they came and never referred to how long it had been since she saw them last, if indeed it was a long time. She appreciated whatever was done for her and made her visitor and benefactor feel like a queen for being so gracious and kind and generous. She made it very easy for people to love her. They wanted to see her again, so they did.

That woman was my mother.

I am not a TV addict myself, in fact, I rarely watch television, but I bless it daily for the pleasure it brought my mother and all shut-ins. I don't know what Mother would have done without her TV families, all the people in the soaps in whose lives she got involved, to say nothing of the hockey and football games she got so excited about.

And she did crossword puzzles and double acrostics until they came out of her ears. Some women knit; my mother puzzled. She had a mind like a steel trap. I guess I can face pain and aging, failing health and weakening flesh. ("Old age," wrote an aunt of mine, "is not for sissies.") But God grant me my wits. And you yours.

You haven't lived all this time for nothing. You have a

125

few foxy things you can still do. If you can't get out and see the world, then you can get the world to come and see you.

Most centres have mobile library services, which include taking books to shut-ins. If you can't get to the library, ask the library to deliver. If you still enjoy reading, you get a bonus, but even if you don't or just want to look at the pictures, at least you have a human being coming to you – bearing books. And if you're blind, the library will bring you tapes of books to listen to, and a cassette player to listen to them. This service is also available by mail in smaller centres through the CNIB. I've read of Talking Book Clubs, as well, something to watch your newspaper for. And while you're at it, do what a lot of younger families are doing. Buy or rent a VCR and rent movies to watch at home. I've seen ads for weekend specials combining pizza and a movie delivered to your door. Share the price with one or two friends and enjoy.

If you have a faith, and most people do, whether or not it bears the title of a religion, you can pray a lot. But if you believe in organized religion as well, you're ahead of the game. Make sure your name is still on the lists of whatever church or temple you belonged to, keep up your dues (offering), and you'll be on the visiting list. That means that once or twice or several times a year some of the more active women of the church will bring you flowers left over from a special service or tea, and the minister might even drop in to check on your spiritual progress – and that all makes for more visitors to darken your doorstep and lighten your life.

Enquire about physiotherapy treatments. You probably need them, anyway. Ask your doctor if he would recommend them. A young physiotherapist coming in once or twice a month can do wonders for your morale as well as your muscles and it doesn't cost you anything. She (he?) is paid by whatever form of medical insurance applies to your province and your age.

Similarly, if you're too weak to wash your own hair now, or need some other specific personal help, you can put in for a Victorian Order Nurse to come on a regular basis to help you out – once or twice a week. The charge for this is nominal and varies according to your ability to pay. And it pays off in more than just a clean head. You'll make another young friend and that's always a pleasure.

There are elderly persons centres in most communities now, usually part of a local community centre, though sometimes separate. Depending on the support they have from federal, provincial, and municipal sources, as well as from volunteers in the community, they offer a variety of services to old people. A volunteer may come and wash a woman's hair, or shave a man, if they lack the strength to do it for themselves. There are regular foot clinics – know why? Because old people are not as supple and have trouble cutting their toenails, among other things. Volunteers will help old people shop, or go to the doctor, or deal with government letters and forms that are often confusing and frightening (bureaucracy always is). And they'll help you with your income tax return, for a nominal fee.

There is usually a nutritionist on staff either at the elderly persons centre or at the local community health centre or public health office in your area. The nutritionist will help you plan your meals for ease of preparation but maximum nutrition and supply you with booklets and pamphlets to help you in your shopping and menu planning. A centre will often conduct a regular weekly gourmet group session, guided by the nutritionist, when a number of elderly people are invited to come and help cook and eat a new dish: food for thought, food for pleasure, and friends to eat it with.

Here's another suggestion, one so simple you'll

laugh. Write letters. Don't laugh. If your hands aren't too sore, if you can spell, and even if you can't, pick up your ballpoint and write. Write away for things. Get free samples. It'll make your mailbox interesting. Write your MP; he/she has to answer – and you don't have to put a stamp on that letter. Write complaints or kudos to manufacturers. They'll answer too, and probably send you more free samples. Find a pen pal. And, of course, if you have distant children and other relatives, be such a good correspondent that if you were playing tennis you'd beat them hollow, the ball is back in their court so fast. Sooner or later, they'll respond, even sons.

All these are things you can do to keep the world coming to you without stirring out of your room. If you have more than a room, and a little more energy, issue some invitations. By this time you know when the bad times are. Reach out to others then. Share a seasonal downer with them and turn it into a high spot. Beat the Anniversary Reaction. Phone a senior citizen's home, if you aren't in one yourself, and invite two or three of the more active women to join you in your kitchen to bake Christmas cookies, or Easter or Hanukkah bread, or whatever. If you can't afford the price of all the ingredients, ask them to chip in. They'll love the chance to putter in a real kitchen again and to have some home-baking to take back to share with their friends, and you have solved another day of the blahs. You can also do this with your grandchildren, should you be so lucky as to (a) have any (b) in the same city or town. But don't expect their mothers to be pleased with the kid's greasy clothes and full tummies when they return home. Grandmothers are notorious for being a bad influence – I think it skips a generation.

Go back to the piano you're sorry you neglected when your parents nagged you to go and practise; read all the books you never had time to get around to; learn a foreign language; take up painting, and think of Grandma Moses! Your work is over. Why not give yourself a treat? In doing so, you are doing yourself and the society you live in the biggest service of all. *You are asserting your right to be here.* In her book *The Second Sex* Simone de Beauvoir deals uncompromisingly with the problem of age for a woman. "When she has given up the struggle against the fatality of time," writes de Beauvoir, "another combat begins: *She must maintain a place on earth.*"

You have to keep on having goals in sight. You were not meant to languish in apathy. God grant you your health and your wits and enough money to keep food on your table and a roof over your head so you can keep on truckin'.

It's never too late, as the saying goes. You need not only spirit and wit and means, you need enough *anger* not to let anyone do you in, let you down, put you off, rub you out. In the old days this anger was, I believe, called backbone. It's backbone that is going to give you the strength to keep on doing your own thing. Heaven knows you have the freedom. This is one of the ironies of widowhood, all along the way, that you have been granted unique freedom.

"Strange that creatures without backbones have the hardest shells," wrote the poet Kahlil Gibran. *You* have backbone, so don't bother acquiring a shell. Stay soft. Stay open. Hang loose, as they say. Don't harden with resentment or self-pity. Don't tyrannize other people with your needs. Don't blackmail your children with your love. A free gift of love is infinitely more valuable. Wait for it. You have all the time in the world.

That's what I keep telling myself. I have all the time in the world, and I do. By the time I'm eighty-five, my marriage is going to seem like an interlude in my life, occupying, as it will have, less than one-quarter of it. No matter at what age you have been widowed, you will have said, "It's too soon," and of course it was. But now you have a lot of time to put in, no matter what age you are. The life expectancy for girls born in 1981 was seventy-nine years, but if a woman has reached the age of thirty-five today, her life expectancy is eighty-one years, and if she is sixty-five today, she has at least another eighteen years to live. I've already mentioned that the average age at which a woman is widowed is fifty-six. So you have a lot of time on your hands. You cannot afford to be less of a person.

The years stretch on ahead, like a long tunnel of time, and what are you going to do with them? After the children have left, after you have retired from your work, and after other women friends have joined your ranks (Welcome to the Club), there remains your own cycle of days to put in before your time is up. Sooner or later, most of us will be aging lonely widows. You can't argue with statistics. The question is: do you have the means to cope with this last challenge life is throwing at you? By "means," I include everything: physical, mental, spiritual, and financial.

You have proved your dogged endurance, your stamina, your innate sense of timing, and your skill at long distances. As you get older why not enjoy it? By this time you have earned a right to your knobs, your nonconformities. You don't have to diet any more – at least not for appearance's sake, though you must guard your health. You can be outspoken and opinionated and eccentric – as long as you remain nice enough to retain your visiting privileges.

"Want to have some fun on your next birthday?" reads a contemporary card. "Paint racing stripes on your cane." I hope this has supplied the paint.

# 10

## Sympathy, haircuts and assorted problems

*What is the world to a man whose wife is a widow?*

*Irish proverb*

People have odd attitudes towards the bereaved, almost as odd as their attitudes towards death. They attend the funeral and bury both halves of the couple – or seemingly so. The sight of a recent widow seems to be too much of a reminder of mortality so they try to avoid her. When they do run into her, usually by accident and not by design, they are oversolicitous about her health. They tell her how fine she is looking.

She isn't. She looks like death warmed over. She hasn't started to eat or sleep with any regularity yet. How can she look like anything but what she is – a lost soul? I could tell when I really started looking better. People stopped telling me I was looking better.

"You're looking better?" they kept saying hopefully,

with a question. As if you'd been sick. And of course you were, sick to your soul.

You have suffered one of the most traumatic blows it is possible to suffer. You may be walking around upright but your mind is still on crutches. Well, don't blame people. I've done the same thing myself, both before and since my husband's death. There is something awe-inspiring, silencing, and shattering about emotional pain that does leave one at a loss for words. Perhaps gestures are better. I've mentioned before my need for hugs. I'm sure other people feel the same way. Human physical comfort, no strings. I saw a cartoon once, no caption, which said it all. It was a vending machine; the sign on it read: "Hugs, 25¢." I wish I could have one installed.

It's not that people lack compassion. I do believe that most people think of themselves as kind and well-meaning. They're busy, they're shy, and they're tactless. So maybe if someone told them how to treat a widow, or anyone who has been recently bereaved, it would help us all. And maybe it would also help the bereaved, because they don't always know what they want and wish someone else would figure it out for them.

Listen. Just listen. More than anything, in the first few weeks of horror following a death, the widow needs someone to listen to her. She has to re-live the death, re-live the life she and her husband shared, begin to establish a new relationship with him and with the world she's still living in. She desperately needs to talk. Give her time. Let her talk.

Talk about him with her. Too many people clam up about the dead. It's not going to make her feel worse to talk about him, it's going to make her feel better. Recall funny things he said, nice things he did, good times you had together. My husband was a very witty man. Some of the nicest sympathy letters I received were ones in which the writer recalled some especially witty line he had said.

Conjure up for her the life she had. She has to confront it, look at it, and eventually start to withdraw. Help her to do so. He is still a living presence to her. She'll stop in time. Probably her own good sense will tell her when. One of the really horrible things I did was to talk about my husband on my first dates with other men. Like nonstop. That was hardly fair. It took me a while to realize what I was doing, and then I shut up. It's a test of others' tolerance and good will, I suppose, but it's a wonder they didn't hand me a memorial candle to light and leave.

Invite her over. But don't just say, "Drop in any time," because she won't come. She's feeling hypersensitive and she may have already suffered a few rebuffs or indications that she's not as welcome as she was when she was part of a couple. One of the nicest things any couple did for me was to ask me to their place for a nightcap frequently after choir rehearsal. I used to dread going home at night after a meeting because there was no one to tell about it and the children were in bed. It's something else you have to get used to.

Another couple used to ask me for a TGIF drink on Fridays, and that made me feel as if weekends weren't all bad.

So be specific in your invitations to a widow. Say when. And it wouldn't hurt to make it for dinner once in a while. That applies for months after the fact. If you're feeling guilty because you haven't done anything about poor Mary Smith, it's never too late. She's still alone. Ask her for dinner, preferably on a night when your husband is home. She won't eat him.

Hang in there. So many people, as I have indicated, drift away. Try for a few months, anyway, to give her some regular time. Maybe you could plan a weekly or monthly shopping excursion, something special, or a visit to an art gallery, or a swim, or a walk in the park – anything, just so it's planned and regular and forces her to think ahead a bit, plan for an event in the future, however simple.

Don't give her unsolicited advice. Don't tell her what to do. Don't make harsh judgements of what she has done. She's supersensitive anyway. If she wants your advice, she'll ask for it. I had one friend, within the week of my husband's death, criticize his insurance provisions for me and my family. What could I do about them then? In any case, they were what we had both agreed upon. We had always planned that I would work if he died early (never thinking that he would), and so we planned for a thin bottom line and spent our money on other things, like travel together. I am grateful for my memories.

Don't save up all the hard luck stories to tell her expecting her to realize that she isn't the only one with problems. She knows that, but she's having enough trouble coping with her own right now. Telling her others doesn't make her feel any better.

I had one friend who, whenever we got together, at one point would nod her head wisely and say sententiously, "There are worse things than death." It was home-truth time, and she wanted me to know how lucky I was that I didn't have a living vegetable tied up to tubes in the hospital, or a human skeleton wasting away with pain in front of my eyes. I know, I know. We are given enough strength, I hope, to bear our own pain. I would not trade with others, nor they with me, in all likelihood. Sufficient unto the day.

Don't say, "You're lucky. You still have your children." It's true, they are blessings. But the widow doesn't feel very lucky and resents being reminded that she still owes a debt of gratitude. She'll come around to it.

Don't say, "He had a long, full life." Not full enough as far as she's concerned, and not nearly long enough. I had one widow, whose husband died at sixty-six, say to me that she felt it was too soon and unfair for him to die so young, forgetting that mine had died at forty-five. Tact takes a lot of practice and we all need it.

Do try to remember whom you're talking to. I ran into one woman in the supermarket shortly after my husband died who started telling me that her husband was away on a business trip and she said, "You know how much you get done when they're away and not underfoot." Yes.

"You're so free-wheeling," exclaimed a friend, commenting on the fact that I had driven myself in and out of Toronto (to a business appointment) in a day. "I wouldn't do that except under duress." Or because there's no alternative.

"You're getting so much thinner," exclaimed the same friend. "I envy you." Envy?

"There's someone you should meet," a friend told me. "She just moved in on the street next to you. You'll have a lot in common. Her husband's dead too." Common denominator?

"I guess the mistletoe isn't much use to you," said a friend at my first Christmas party A.D., "all the men here are married."

Don't say, "Cheer up – maybe next time you'll marry a rich husband." I know one widow to whom this was said at graveside. It was six months before someone said it to me. It's such a classic gaffe, I couldn't believe it was actually being said and I laughed out loud.

Don't ask, right after the interment, if she wants to sell the house. Someone asked my mother during my father's terminal illness. Even vultures have the tact to circle a while before they land.

Don't tell her all your troubles with your husband,

135

with the implication that she's lucky she's well out of it. She'll sympathize with your daily concerns, but she doesn't want a glimpse of husband-wife relations, not for a while.

And don't, don't, tell her how importunate your husband is in the bedroom. I can remember being almost sick with pain when a couple of friends started discussing their husbands' sexual behaviour ("He's at me all the time, never leaves me alone"). That's dirty pool.

And, men (we're back to sex again, I'm afraid), don't figure on giving her a treat. But an arm on a shoulder or a friendly hug is okay.

Try, if you can, to remember anniversaries, or at least one milestone in her year. If something aids you in remembering her husband's death date, then write her a note or phone her or send her a rose the following year. She hasn't forgotten what day it is. Or, if you were close, and enjoyed celebrating their wedding anniversary with them, remember it with her. Say something. It won't bring up any pain she might not have experienced. It comforts her that you also miss him and remember the good times.

Remember the good times and the good friends. If I have sounded harsh or critical of some of the treatment I've had, please understand that these were exceptions. As one widow said to me when she found out I was writing a book about widowhood, "Be sure to write about friends." Yes. Where would any of us be without them? I count among my richest blessings the friends who supported and cared for me, and continue to do so, in my loneliness and pain. They think of ways to help me that I could never think of myself. They also think of turning up at moments of need.

And sometimes it's surprising who turns up. The old saying, "You find out who your friends are," is true. Old old friends, of course, remain friends, steadfast and true.

But sometimes new friends, people you thought were friends, turn out to have been couple-friends, or convenience-friends, or reciprocal-friends, and when you are no longer part of a couple, when it is no longer convenient to know you, or when you are less able to reciprocate favours or invitations, these people fall away. On the other hand, you will find to your surprise that some of the people whom you thought of as very friendly acquaintances, but not close, become your staunchest supporters and most thoughtful allies. You never know.

One of the most delightful therapeutic things that was done for me happened after I moved to my new home in Toronto. I was invited, by two couples whom I knew well but not intimately, to join their Gourmet Dinner Club. It seems they had suffered several separations in their ranks, and they decided there was as much continuity in a single with a floating partner as there was in a couple with a precarious marriage. I had never recovered my interest in cooking since Bill died. Having to plan menus and suggest recipes to the group, and also, of course, to produce again, was marvellous therapy. It lured me back into the kitchen. Another rule: Help her to find an interest.

Remember that the times when married people are most occupied, widows are probably unoccupied, particularly in the early months. I can remember sitting quietly in my living room early one Saturday evening in June, some six weeks A.D., with soft tears streaming down my face. Someone came whom I didn't know that well, but whom I liked. And we talked. And became better friends.

I remembered the timing and did exactly the same thing for a fresh widow later that fall. And made another friend.

Another time, just before the Stratford Festival opening, which always gives me an Anniversary Reaction, another seemingly remote friend dropped in with some flowers from her garden. And we talked.

If you're too far away to risk a drop-in call, then phone. Say, "Just thought I'd call," and take it from there. You can never go wrong by taking a little thought. And it's never too late. One widow warned me that the second year is in many ways as bad or worse than the first because people think you must be over it by now and withdraw some of their support. She's still alone.

If you're going to a meeting or a dinner or something that you know the widow will be going to as well, ask her if she wants a lift. Sometimes she gets stubborn (I did) and proud and won't ask for help. But she hopes like hell someone else will think of it. I went to my daughter's high school graduation exercises alone because I would not ask to go with anyone, and no one thought of asking me to go with them. I guess that's how I learned to go alone to things. It's either that, or stay at home.

People are wonderful in times of stress. They rally round when there's a death or a serious illness. Then they are kindness itself and they know what to do. But they – we – all tend to forget the dailiness of loneliness and the unrelenting pressure of having to do everything yourself. An occasional thought on a day that isn't special will be greatly appreciated and makes the load seem lighter. Try not to forget her in the daily rush.

A lot of these rules apply to both widows and widowers. There are some differences between them and it might help to consider them.

A widow is going to have trouble with maintenance and home repair. If you're a male friend and happen to be handy, ask her if there's anything that needs fixing, or take a look around for yourself. One neighbour of ours noticed that some tiles had dropped off our pool and, without being asked, got some caulking mixture and replaced them. Wow.

138

A widower, on the other hand, is having trouble coping with the meals. Even if he has very young children and has a housekeeper, you can bet the standards aren't as high as they used to be. Take over a fresh pie, warm from your oven, or a cake, or home-baked bread.

Tell a widower, as tactfully as you can, when his hair needs cutting. Chances are it was his wife who reminded him and she's not around to do it.

Ask him and his family to dinner. This applies to anyone, doesn't it? Breaking bread together is a comforting thing to do. It seems to assert normality, to say, as nothing else does, that life does go on. We all have to eat.

A widower told me he could fix a kettle but he couldn't select his own ties. He can clean the house all right but what's he going to do when a chair needs recovering, and he can't figure out what colour it should be? He can cook a roast beef but he can't plan a week's menus and therefore he has trouble with the shopping list.

A widow, on the other hand, has trouble with fuses, car maintenance, and hanging pictures.

Both widow and widower are disoriented, and for much longer than you realize. They go through the motions of normality; they go about what remains of their lives and their business and they seem to be making normal responses to the demands of daily life. But they are only half there. They are conducting a constant inner dialogue with someone who is absent. They are stanching a wound that has torn a gaping hole in their psyches. They are suffering withdrawal symptoms of the most severe kind.

So what can you do? Don't withdraw from them. Give them your support and sympathy. Say you're sorry, and prove it.

# 11

## Plan ahead

*A man called on me the other day with the idea of insuring my life. Now I detest life insurance agents; they always argue that I shall some day die, which is not so.*

Stephen Leacock

All right, you've been through it. Now, if *you* died last night, would your executor/trix have all the information he/she needed to make life easier for your survivors? Do you, in fact, have an executor? Have you made out a will?

If you were going away on a trip and leaving children behind, you'd leave instructions for the baby-sitter, wouldn't you? Rather complete ones, in fact, with the doctor's phone number, and the numbers of the plumber, TV and washer repair men, and possibly even some suggested menus, and a plan of action. Consider your death, then, merely as a bigger trip with this exception: no one can reach you where you're going. They can't ask you questions then, so answer them before you go.

Few people leave adequate information. Somehow they seem to feel that preparation is like an invitation. It isn't. It's a kindness you can perform for your children or whoever you leave behind. It's not only the financial arrangements that you've made that others have to know about, it's also the fiddley details that no one else knows but you. You might even go so far as to plan your own funeral. I had an aunt who did that. Wrote her own obituary, too.

First the business. Take several sheets of paper and begin your list. You do have a will, don't you? One copy should be with your lawyer and one with you. Write down where it is. (Don't put your will or your life insurance policies in a safety deposit box because it will be sealed on your death and they must be immediately accessible.) List your policies, life, disability, fire, automobile, house, etc., and indicate where they may be found. List your bank accounts and say where your passbooks are. Write down anything, everything you have: bonds, stocks, trust certificates, Retirement Savings Plans, deeds, mortgages, contracts, names of any business partners and all papers connected with business arrangements. And tell where they are. Plus your tax returns, financial statements, guarantees and warranties on your possessions (such as stove, car etc.). Where are the car keys and the car ownership registration? Where is the safety deposit box located and where is the key to it?

It would be a very good idea to write down the purchase price of any stocks you own, and the date of purchase, and the maturity dates of bonds, and the expiry dates of guaranteed investment certificates. List your future financial obligations and decisions, such as mortgage payments or stock options. Or tell what your rent is and when it's due. Is there a series of post-dated cheques outstanding on that? And make a list of any other post-dated cheques you may have written.

Include receipts that would be required to make up your final income tax return, as well as income statements, and don't forget information concerning capital gains or losses. Write down a list of any gifts made, trusts established, charitable gifts (or obligations).

Now list the locations of any stored valuables like jewellery, furs, stamp collections. You might like to talk over with your children the disposition of some of your possessions. Maybe one of them has always secretly loved a particular ornament or painting and would love to have it. Find out now, and reach an agreement about it, verbal or written. Written is better.

List your credit cards and their location, including the duplicates. And don't forget your birth certificate and your Social Insurance card – no one can do a thing without them. Tell where the bills are kept, and list any outstanding debts, including contractual obligations such as cable TV, snow removal contracts, decorating contracts, things on order. List your current and ongoing expenses. List your book club memberships and magazine subscriptions so that something can be done about them. And any club memberships.

Nothing is more baffling than a bunch of keys whose locks are unknown. As a matter of fact, keys paralyze me. I have keys that are meaningless to me now but that somehow I'm afraid to throw away. I have a key that I think belongs to a locker I used when I was at university. If I ever go back in a time machine it could be useful. When I travel I never lock my luggage because I can't identify the keys to any of my bags. I'm not recommending that you harbour unidentified keys. The ideal thing would be to label them. If you're so organized you already have, you don't need to read a list like this.

Tell where your appointment book is and make sure someone will be aware of any appointments you have that have to be cancelled. My husband had just begun a series with a dentist which I had to cancel. Does anyone know similar information about you? You should also have a record of your children's appointments and lessons so that they may be continued (or postponed as the occasion dictates). Do any of your children have a refillable prescription? Where is it? What about their eyes? Where is the correction prescription? Where do you buy their glasses? Where are their birth certificates, passports, school records, medical records? Do any of them have bank accounts or trust funds established for them? Have they had special bequests from grandparents or from your husband that they don't know about? Obviously these questions apply more to younger children, but older ones don't always know everything about themselves, their business and possessions. Are there any insurance policies on them? I used to take out school insurance on my children each year. If you do that, you'll have to say where those papers are.

If you have any obligations to other relatives, say so. I'm thinking of women who may contribute some support to an aged parent, or who are helping out a child on his own. In the case of the children, the support will likely continue since they will be beneficiaries of any life insurance you may hold, and will inherit your estate. But what about a parent? I am told that it is possible for a widow to buy a contract called a "joint and last survivor annuity," usually on a two-thirds, one-third basis, that is, two-thirds of it riding on your life, and one-third of it riding on the life of the person you want to take care of. It can, however, be determined in any proportion you see fit, in terms of the amount of money you're talking about. This will enable you to continue payments to a parent or in-law in the event of your death. It's very cheap because the odds are against your parent outliving you, quite bluntly. This kind of protection can also be arranged for a handicapped sibling or child, but it's much more expensive because the odds are different.

The youngest of my four children, Matthew, is learning disabled and epileptic. When my other three children were all in university, I took out term insurance on my life naming Matthew as sole beneficiary. That way, I figured that if I died suddenly within the next four or five years, there would be enough money to set up care for Matthew without disrupting his brother's and sisters' lives. At the same time, let me assure you, I take very good care of my children's only parent.

Now start listing names, addresses, and telephone numbers. Start with your lawyer, life insurance agent, casualty agent, accountant, banker, broker, and any other financial advisors you may have. Include your and your children's doctors, dentist, pediatrician, orthodontist, speech therapist – all the people you can think of that you have dealings with. It's a good idea to include the names of teachers, Scout leaders, maybe even a few of your children's close friends. And why not include your maintenance people: plumber, washer repairman, cleaning lady, etc. Who else? Your children know who your friends are, or do they?

Tell them where your Christmas card list is, or your address book, or both. They'll need names and addresses to inform distant relatives (distant geographically, that is) and friends of your death. And a Christmas card list is a handy source of names for pallbearers, if that's the kind of funeral you want. Or you can pick your own pallbearers, and write them down. Include a few alternates, in case some of them go before you do. And while you're at it, include an alternate executor/trix for the same reason. Did you know you can stipulate that your executor receive a fee for services rendered? If you've made a deal with someone to take the children, write that down too, though that's probably in your will.

If all this paperwork doesn't appeal to you, find a memory aid for keeping track of your possessions. Banks, insurance and investment companies often publish useful pamphlets. List all your fiddleys: the deed to a cemetery plot, if any; bank and investment accounts; outstanding debts or loans; insurance papers; your will. Give a copy to your executor.

One more thing. What about the funeral? Funerals are primitive but they are for the living, not the dead. It took me a while to figure that out. Other people really do need to pay some physical heed to the passing of one from their midst, some nodding of the head, dabbing of the eyes, some salute, some farewell. A funeral with its attendant ritual and ceremony gives the immediate family some opportunity to begin the work of confrontation and withdrawal and provides a social event by which relatives and friends gather round and offer some comfort for what it's worth. Sometimes it's worth a lot.

Funerals have been much maligned lately. The high cost of dying has been the subject of a great deal of criticism, and ridicule has been hurled at the pussy-footing euphemisms of funeral parlance: The Loved One is resting in The Slumber Room. Satin-quilted caskets and embalming and grave liners are all part of the euphemistic approach to death. They are also part of the emotional blackmail people tend to get caught up in at a time like death. A high-class (read expensive) funeral always costs more than The Departed would have spent.

Funerals have changed very little in format in this century. They're still stuffy and mid-Victorian. When you think how weddings have changed, with the partic-ipants writing their own vows, choosing their own blessings, prayers and music, and even location, you realize how backward funerals are. Few people plan their own funerals. Maybe we'd have some better ones if they did. I heard of a memorial service held for a young priest which was a real celebration of his life. People stood up and remembered things about him; tapes were played of the best words from his sermons; the Toronto Dance Company, which he had used in his life for his services, performed at his memorial tribute.

You could do that too, if you planned ahead. I wish I'd thought of some of these things before Bill died.

Since his death, I have discovered that not all the people I once knew are in graveyards. Before, the only one I knew about who wasn't was the poet Pauline Johnson – her ashes are buried in Stanley Park in British Columbia. But here are some other picturesque resting places I have learned since. One friend whose home is beside an artificial lake put her husband's ashes in a thicket of trees on the other side of the lake from the house, all in view of her picture window. The actor Leslie Yeo told me that his wife Hilary Vernon's ashes are under a tree in the lovely farmyard garden of actress Pat Galloway and her husband Dr. Bernhard Frischke. The ashes of Reverend Russell D. Horsburgh are buried in the crawl space under the exact centre of the sanctuary of Zion United Church in Hamilton. There is a plaque on the wall attesting to this fact.

Now why didn't I think of something like that?

As it was, I was very traditional. I was taken to pick a double plot in Stratford cemetery, and my husband lies on the stage-right side. I bought a large grey marble stone with his name and birth date and death date on it – $500 plus tax. I was reminded of the line "nothing's certain but death and taxes." Very appropriate to tax tombstones. For a little more I could have had my name and birth date put on it – a very popular custom there – all filled out but the last piece of information. I declined, saying I might drown in the South Seas and my body never be recovered, and that would be a terrible waste of stone-cutting. I honestly don't like that empty space waiting for me. Every time one of my kids gets sick I think maybe they'll beat me to that space. That's morbid.

Even during the neuter time of my post-amputative recovery I wrote in my diary: "If I ever marry again, whose wife will I be when I die and where will I be buried?" And the real cruncher is that I'm a terrible gardener. Every time I go and look at the sad geraniums I put in each year and the struggling Japanese yews I planted I say to my husband: "Well, you always knew what a terrible gardener I am."

One widow I know found herself washed up on a more alien shore than mine. She and her four children left Ohio after her husband suddenly died. She knew she would never return. She bought a single plot, one small marker, took a picture of it, and moved back to Canada with her kids.

Bodies take up a lot of space in graveyards. Some big cities and small islands have resorted to stacking. But the green spaces cemeteries provide are like oases in the concrete jungles that many of our cities have become, one of the few places where people can find some peace and quiet, one of the few places, indeed, that people still pray, outside of a church. Emotions still hover around the plot, no matter how much you may tell yourself your loved one isn't there, that it's just his earthly remains that are deposited.

My own emotions were both raw and ambivalent, I can see now, both toward the cemetery and the tombstone. It has taken me some time to recover my perspective and to acknowledge the value and need of these taboo symbols of our society. They are associated with death in our minds and we prefer not to think of them.

But we forget the very real pleasure and education people get from wandering in cemeteries and reading old tombstones. We get a sense of history and sociology from them, some idea of the average lifespan of an earlier generation, some hint of the anguish parents suffered in the loss of children to diphtheria or polio, and of the pain men suffered losing their wives in childbirth. (Modern medicine and antisepsis have changed the stories that tombstones tell.) If we cease to put up tombstones, and tombstones not only with dates but with bits of poetry and wry comments and details about the life or death of the person thus commemorated, future generations will lose a portion of our history that they are entitled to have. It's only fair that our posterity should be able to walk in quiet green spaces and puzzle over our marble memoirs and wonder about us. I want them to.

There is a lot to be said for cremation. Unfortunately for me, it wasn't said before my husband died. Everything I've learned since then has been the hard way. I think it has to be handled very carefully. Scattered ashes cannot be visited. And as I have rethought visiting cemeteries, so I have rethought scattering. Perhaps you, too, should give it some mind-time.

If we're going to talk about cremation, why not talk about transplants and the whole medical science of spare parts? Whether the remains are going to be burned or buried, there is no earthly reason why you shouldn't donate any good usable pieces so that others may live. Quite a lot of a human being can be recycled now, about twenty-five different bits, as a matter of fact, including the kidneys, bones and joints, bone marrow, corneas, brains, heart, lungs, livers, intestines (for research), pancreas, temporal bones (in the ear), pituitary glands, and skin. God knows, you won't be using them where you're going, and if you do, He'll look after it. If you retain some sort of vague idea about the literal resurrection of the body, that's all right, too. You don't have to worry. If Judgement Day really is a literal one-time event (I have a theory about it occurring all the time on a time-warp) with all the people who ever lived brought together at the same time, the spare parts and the ashes will certainly be reassembled as well. If God can handle the traffic problem, He can do anything, and He *can* do anything. Consider giving your parts to a good cause – another human being.

I wish I had discussed this with my husband, but I can do something about me at least. Why don't *you* take time now and think about it? Think it through. The government of Ontario has made a consent form available to every driver. It's on the back of the driver's licence and has space to indicate what parts you're willing to spare in case of a fatal accident. It's a shame to let them go to waste. You can enquire whether your province has a similar provision or ask what your local hospitals are doing.

Even if you give your body to science or to other people, it won't all be used, so you can't ignore the problem. You still have to decide how to deal with what's left, and you should allow for the emotions of your survivors. Perhaps they would like to plant a flower on you or water your grave with the odd tear. Talk it over with them. It might save you or them some money, too. A no-name, generic funeral costs from $500 to $1,000, while a slightly more elaborate one can run $1,500 to $2,800 (GST and crematorium or cemetery charges not included). You can cut a few corners by asking for the cheapest casket, skipping the grave liner, and requesting no embalming, but you may get an argument from the funeral director, especially on the last item. One funeral director told me why:

"Most funeral homes are manned 24 hours a day (another reason for the costs), this means someone lives there; you can't stick the body in the garage for three or four days! Embalming can or may be necessary even in cases of closed casket to protect the public coming into the funeral home and the funeral director from one of the unpleasant aspects of death."

Viewing the body, I am told, is very important. It begins the grief work for everyone. You have to see it to believe it. Certainly that's true for the immediate family. I'm not so sure that it's necessary or even desirable for "outsiders" to see the body; it is, finally, a matter of personal preference. It was one thing I knew for sure what my husband's opinion was. He had sounded off only a short time before his death on how much he hated an open casket. So I closed his – *after* our private family service.

There are four basic services provided by a funeral home:

1. moving the body,
2. embalming the body,
3. supplying a casket (a casket is not required for cremation),
4. providing the facilities of the funeral home for viewing and/or the ceremony.

The general services of the funeral director are included in the overall fee. You can get an itemized list of goods and services, and you can get prices over the phone so that you need not be trapped by emotion and inertia once you're in the funeral home.

But if the high cost of dying worries you, why not investigate memorial societies? More than 250,000 Canadians have joined this kind of Price Club for funerals. One-time membership fees vary across Canada but average thirty-five dollars for the first family member, and twenty-five dollars for second and subsequent members. With your membership card you will receive a handbook that lists all the funeral, burial, and cremation options with prices; and a form for you to record your wishes. One copy goes on file with your funeral home of choice; one goes to your family or executor; one stays with you.

If that's what you want. Some people want pomp and panoply. I had an aunt, the one who wrote her own obituary, who demanded the most expensive casket available. She said she'd never had a Cadillac in her lifetime so she wanted a Cadillac of coffins when she died. She got it.

But my funeral director friend takes exception to my expression "pomp and panoply" and to my reference to a Cadillac of coffins. He reports to me the following statistics: "25 per cent of the public want either a concrete vault or an airtight casket (Cadillac?); 94 per cent said they would like a funeral service; 100 per cent of widows said they would use a funeral home again; 96 per cent of widows said there was an adequate selection of funeral types; 91 per cent of the public attend a friend's funeral; 86 per cent say they want their friends and relatives around at a time of loss; 72 per cent say a religious service helps." In short, we the public are very traditional.

Perhaps I have done undertakers a grave injustice, if you'll pardon the pun. Certainly we need to *do* something to acknowledge the passing of someone from our midst, and we need help to do it. No one would argue with that. To leave life certainly requires a proper goodbye, and a proper goodbye gives everyone a chance to shake down and realize that a departure has taken place.

Then, too, the lead car behind the hearse is as close as you can get to an acknowledgment of your own mortality. Next time up, it's your turn. It's not all bad to face that fact.

And funerals and cemeteries also provide comfort in a tangible way. The survivors get to *do* something for the one who has died. We all know the soul has gone on, but we respect and handle with care the earthly temple of that dear soul – yes, even if we reduce it to ashes. I carried my mother's ashes back to be buried beside my father, and I carried that dear burden under my heart with love and pain.

Love doesn't die with the body. We need ways to express our love even after the body is no longer present. That's why Jewish people sit shiva – a wonderful custom! – and the Irish are noted for their wakes. Attention must be paid.

Most people think they're immortal, until it's proved otherwise. This seeming inability to envision one's own death, coupled with a general shrinking from the subject on the part of society at large, leaves most people completely unprepared for death, whether it's sudden or after a prolonged illness. As a matter of fact, in the case of a diagnosed terminal illness, the silence can often be worse. I know several widows and one widower who maintained, by some sort of mutual tacit agreement, complete silence about the impending death of their respective spouses. Neither party was willing to call a spade a spade, let alone acknowledge the imminent need to dig a grave with one.

Death is the only obscenity left in our society, the taboo that everyone still observes. I suppose it's fear of the unknown. But you and I know, don't we?

I'm not afraid of dying and death. It's living that's hard.

# 12

## Help is on the way

*God help those who do not help themselves.*

*Addison Mizner*

This is a do-it-yourself age we live in. Books and courses abound in self-help projects ranging from furniture upholstery to self-hypnosis. The magazines and newspapers are full of advice about anything that's troubling you, from dry skin to weekend guests, and they give short courses in everything from dog-training to balancing a budget. Entire bookstores are devoted to nothing but how-to and can-do books. There are information services provided by just about every business you can name, with pamphlets available on request.

So?

You might be the most competent person in the whole world, and you certainly know how to read directions, but you can't help feeling paralyzed when it's all laid on your shoulders – everything, all the maintenance, all the decisions, everything. And there are times when you just don't know where to turn, who to ask, how to find the answers you need.

What you need first is the sure and certain knowledge that you are going to survive. It said that in the newspaper, didn't it? "He is survived by his wife." Your back may be against the wall; you may be driven to tears, but you will not be driven to total collapse. And even if you are, well, there's help for that, too.

Your very survival is one of life's ironies. More than one widow has said to me, "Isn't it ironic that I had to lose my husband to find myself?" People have said that to me, commenting on my second trajectory career as a writer, wondering whether I capitalized unfairly on my husband's death. Bill always used to say if you get a lemon, make lemonade. If I had my druthers, I'd ruther he were alive and well and still with me. But he's not.

I can't begin to give you all the information you need, but I can give you the reassurance. You will find a way out of this maze of pain and bewilderment. Everyone has a different weak spot, but there are ways of compensating for it.

I get paralyzed by things I have to do that I call "fiddleys" – time-consuming, annoying, unproductive, fiddley details that have to be looked after. I have a friend who feels the same way I do. Know what she did? She hired a college student on a part-time basis, so much an hour, to do her fiddleys for her. She spends less on that than she would pay a cleaning lady, and she doesn't mind cleaning her own house. Her part-time organizer has done things like this for her: renewed her passport, taken inventory of her possessions for insurance evaluation, ordered her children's winter underwear, returned things that aren't suitable. None of these things is difficult, but all are fiddley. My friend is much more relaxed now.

Every once in a while when I am in danger of going down in a sea of paper, I hire a student to come and make sense of my files for me. Thirty hours of sorting and filing can make a new woman of me!

The most fiddley thing I have to do each year is work on my income tax. It really is fiddley because I am a free-lance writer and my income derives from a lot of different sources. I also have fiddley expenses that must be kept track of, like parking and postage, paper and books, and typewriter ribbon (and now floppy disks!), and all stuff like that. I bought a cheap calculator, at my son's suggestion, to help me put my receipts in order before I go to a tax accountant. Some widows I know say they feel a real thrill of accomplishment when they work out their own income-tax forms. I'd go to jail before I achieved that thrill. I choose to use the help available. One tax credit I might not discover pays for the accountant's services, and I claim for his services, too.

If you have other financial problems, there are experts around to talk to you, besides books and bro-chures to read, and courses to take. Your banker doesn't charge; maybe he or she is the one to start with. Talk to a friend or friend's husband who you think knows what he's doing (but don't ask for a private consultation). If you do have to go to a lawyer or a professional consul-tant, just remember that his or her rates per hour are high, so do your homework as I do for my accountant. Prepare your material, your questions, and your infor-mation so that you will use as little as possible of that expensive professional time in the briefing before you ask your questions. You will then be paying for expertise and not for paperwork.

If you have a job problem, you're not alone – but that's no help. At a certain level of education and skill, there are head-hunter organizations that will help you find a job in your field, for a fee. In the past few years there have been waiting lists for the lower-paid, unskilled jobs, which are not too rewarding when you get them. You may need more than advice; you may need training to bring your skills up to a higher paying level. There are resources in each community that you can turn to for guidance. Don't forget the biggest resource you have is yourself, your own determination and spirit.

Look up Human Resources Development Canada (the new name for Canada Employment) in the Blue Pages of your telephone book and phone or drop in. Ask about career planning and workplace information and pick up any free publications available. Affirmative action in hiring is supposed to offer equal job access for women and visible minorities. Private women's networks may be of some help to you.

If you already have a job and are having trouble, go to the personnel officer in the company, or if it's too personal a problem, talk it over with a trusted friend. I have heard of a few large companies that have recognized the stress of bereavement and that conduct workshops to help their employees over this bad time. You might even suggest it in your firm.

What you have to have is a positive attitude. *Of course*, this problem can be solved. *Of course*, you're going to solve it. You solved the last one, didn't you? Each time you solve a problem successfully, it gives you that much more confidence for the next one. That's what I keep telling myself, but someone keeps thinking up new problems!

If you really can't cope, if the world is too much with you, and you feel too discouraged and bogged down to carry on, you could go to your doctor. But don't accept a course of tranquillizers without attempting a long-term solution to your problem. Treat the cause, not the symptom. Go to your minister or rabbi, or make an appointment with a counselor, or get your doctor to refer you to a psychiatrist if things are really bad. It wouldn't hurt to pray.

Some organizations and services that a widow may find helpful are self-explanatory and fairly easy to find, such as the Big Brothers or Big Sisters, or the local chapter of Parents Without Partners. Just keep asking questions.

Self-help groups are most effective. A widow-to-widow program was first developed by the Harvard Medical School, modelled after the Widows' Consultation Center in New York. It has been discovered that another widow is the surest, most effective aid a widow can have. The old line "you have to have been there to know what it's like" is so true it hurts. No one but another widow can reassure you that you are not going insane, and that you will survive. Often a widow will launch a group or service within her own community, creating the lifeline that she needs herself. If there isn't such an organization where you live, perhaps you are the one who will start one to reach out and help others after you. But ask around first, and find out if there is a widows' group in your community.

Churches, YS, and community service organizations as well as enterprising individuals across the country are beginning to recognize the very real needs of the bereaved and to take the responsibility for meeting them. Grief and loneliness are legacies of bereavement that must be faced and treated. Nothing is quite so difficult when there is sympathy, practical help, a chance to communicate one's feelings, and guidance along the way.

Don't be afraid to ask for help. Yelp and holler a little. *Someone* will hear.

# Bibliography

Ariès, Philippe. *The Hour of Our Death*. New York: Knopf, 1981.

Baker, Maureen. *Families: Changing Trends in Canada*. 3rd ed. Toronto: McGraw-Hill Ryerson Ltd., 1996. (Some excellent material on lone-parent families)

The Beardstown Ladies' Investment Club, with Leslie Whitaker. *The Beardstown Ladies' Common-Sense Investment Guide*. New York: Hyperion, 1994.

Buckman, Dr. Robert. *I Don't Know What to Say: How to Help and Support Someone Who is Dying*. Toronto: Key Porter Books, 1988.

Dohaney, M. T. *When Things Get Back to Normal*. Porters Lake, N.S.: Pottersfield Press, 1989.

Dowling, Colette. *The Cinderella Complex*. New York: Pocket Books, Simon & Schuster, 1981.

Friedan, Betty. *The Fountain of Age*. New York: Simon & Schuster, 1993.

Kübler-Ross, Elisabeth. *Death: The Final Stage of Growth*. New York: Touchstone/Simon & Schuster, 1986.

Lewis, C. S. *A Grief Observed*. London: Faber & Faber, 1961.

Lindbergh, Anne Morrow. *Hour of Gold, Hour of Lead.* 1970. Reprint. San Diego and New York: Harcourt Brace Jovanovich, 1993.

Linn, Erin. *150 Facts About Grieving Children.* Incline Village, Nevada: The Publisher's Mark, 1990.

Lukas, Christopher, and Henry M. Seiden. *Silent Grief: Living in the Wake of Suicide.* New York: Bantam Books, 1990.

Marris, Peter. *Loss and Change.* Garden City, N.Y.: Anchor Books, 1975.

Moffat, Mary Jane, ed. *In the Midst of Winter: Selections from the Literature of Mourning.* New York: Vintage Books/Random House, 1982.

Pincus, Lily. *Death and the Family: The Importance of Mourning.* New York: Vintage Books/Random House, 1984.

Steinem, Gloria. *Revolution from Within: A Book of Self-Esteem.* Toronto: Little, Brown and Company, 1992.

Wells, Rosemary. *Helping Children Cope with Grief.* London: Sheldon Press, 1988.

Wylie, Betty Jane. *Reading Between the Lines: The Diaries of Women.* Toronto: Key Porter Books, 1995.

——. *Life's Losses: Living through Grief, Bereavement and Sudden Change.* Toronto: Macmillan Canada, 1996.

——. *Solo Chef.* Toronto: Macmillan Canada, 1997.

——. *Something Might Happen.* Windsor: Black Moss Press, 1989. (Poetry dealing with loss)

——, and Christopher Cottier. *The Best Is Yet to Come: Enjoying a Financially Secure Retirement.* Toronto: Key Porter Books, 1996.

——, and Lynne MacFarlane. *Everywoman's Money Book.* Toronto: Key Porter Books, 1995.

Yaccato, Joanne Thomas. *The Balancing Act: A Canadian Woman's Financial Survival Guide.* Scarborough, ON: Prentice Hall Canada, Inc., 1994.

**Resources**

The following booklets are available free for the asking from

> The Canadian Life and Health Insurance
> Association, Inc.
> One Queen Street East, Suite 1700
> Toronto, ON  M5C 2X9

> *A Guide to Buying Life Insurance*
> *Disability Insurance*

> Call The Information Centre free of charge from
> anywhere in Canada: 1-800-268-8099.

Statistics Canada keeps ahead of social trends with valuable analyses of the data it collects. The books are pricey because statistics are work-intensive, but they're well worth it. Take a look at some of these:

> *Women in Canada, A Statistical Report*, 3rd Edition,
> 1995
> *Women in the WorkPlace*, 2nd Edition, 1993
> *The Living Arrangements of Canada's Older Women*,
> 1982 (out of print, but see if you can find this one in
> a library)

> Statistics Canada
> Ottawa, ON  K1A 0T6

Check your provincial reference centre. Toll-free access in all provinces and territories for users who reside outside the local directory area of any of the regional reference centres.

Check also with The Advisory Council on the Status of Women for material you might find useful. One of my favourites, *Women and Aging*, is probably long since out of print (1978), but it applies to us.

CACSW
National Office
110 O'Connor Street, 9th floor
Ottawa, ON  K1P 5R5

Phone: 613-992-4796

Seniors' magazines are popping up like dandelions all over the country. The best one by far is a national publication for "50-plus lifestyles," published every other month. A $3.00 subscription to the magazine is included with a $10 membership in the Canadian Association of Retired People, but you can get the magazine separately if you wish. Watch particularly for the annual Special Financial Guide for the 50-Plus.

CARP*News*
27 Queen St. E., Ste. 702
Toronto, ON  M5C 2M6

Phone: 416-363-5562

Revenue Canada offers free of charge *The Guide to Preparing Returns for Deceased Persons*, which includes information on filing deadlines, procedures, and the forms required. Executors have until April 30 the following year to file a return. For people who have died after November 30, Revenue Canada allows six months to file.

# Index